DOMINATION

B J Alpha

Copyright © 2025 by B J Alpha

All rights reserved.

No part of this book may be reproduced in any form or by any electronic or mechanical means, including information storage and retrieval systems, without written permission from the author, except for the use of brief quotations in a book review.

This book is a work of fiction. Characters, names, places and incidents are products of the authors imagination or used fictitiously.

Any similarity to actual events, locations or persons living or dead is purely coincidental.

Without in any way limiting the author's exclusive rights under copyright, any use of this publication to "train" generative artificial intelligence (AI) technologies to generate text is expressly prohibited. The author reserves all rights to license uses of this work for generative AI training and development of machine learning language models. No audio files can be produced without the authors written consent beforehand.

Published by: Alpha Team Publishing.

Photographer: Wander Aguiar.

Model: Wander Aguiar.

Edited by: Dee Houpt.

Proofread by: Dee Houpt.

Vinny

I am the don of our Mafia family.

I'm controlling and a ruthless savage, but above all, I'm dominant—inside and outside the bedroom.

I've spent my entire life using people as I see fit, never keeping a woman around for anything more than to satisfy my needs. They become pets, that way they're clear on where I stand and they sit.

When my stepson leaves his daughter and grandchild in my care, everything changes in an instant.

They belong to me despite her telling me otherwise.

When my world becomes too much for her and her secrets are revealed, can I make the ultimate sacrifice and give her the part of me I've kept hidden? Or will my need to dominate every situation be the end of the best little pet to ever happen to me?

NOTE FROM AUTHOR

This book contains sensitive subject matters, tropes and content that some readers may find unsuitable.

Please see my website for full details.

NOTE FROM AUTHOR

You're about to step into a world of domination.

Where the Daddy of all daddies wants to control every part of you.

When you turn the page, be prepared, Daddy Vinny makes his sons look like amateurs in a world where addiction, possession, and deception are welcomed red flags.

You're about to become dominated in the best way possible.

A message to readers…

"Spread the page like a good little pet, and let Daddy take care of you."

- Vinny

Prologue

Vinny

Scanning the crowd, I sigh heavily, then plaster on a smile to all the guests for participating in this evening's festivities. It's my Marino family annual Halloween party, and each year, the costumes are more extravagant than the last.

Even the mayor and numerous members of the local police department have upped their game with their elaborate costumes.

An event like tonight has me on high alert, waiting on bated breath for enemies to strike. I lock eyes with my son Rafael—the oldest of my four boys—and when he lifts his chin, I give him a stern nod. Becoming a young father was always my future, it was expected of me, yet it's only now that I'm grateful for it. It's allowed me to keep control of the family business, to train my sons in the skills they need while giving me the privilege to witness my grandchildren growing.

At fifty-five, I still have decades left in me despite the fact Rafael is itching to reign as the don.

Life in the Mafia is different from the outside world, much different, and while many people don't understand it, I don't give a fuck. We do things our way.

That's why I don't dress up for the party, and until recently, my boys didn't either. Although, Ellie, Rafael's wife, clings to a mask he wore earlier in the evening, proving my son has made some effort, if only a little. My gaze travels over her school uniform, but I quickly divert my focus. The girl was barely eighteen when he coaxed her to become his son's nanny, and it's clear he has a thing for the uniform; it's not the first time I've seen her in it. I don't need an explanation of their dynamic. It's an obvious one and not something I intend to get involved in. Besides, my sons were raised in a liberal household, they understand that sex is just that, sex. And yet, three of my sons claim to have found something more, something I haven't. A connection, love.

My right-hand man, Massio, draws my attention as he strides toward me with purpose, and when he whispers into my ear, I almost consider having that hearing test my youngest son continues to taunt me with. "Robert's not here this year," he grinds out, and I narrow my eyes.

When my stepson, Robert, made an appearance at a Halloween party a few years ago, I instructed my staff to start keeping tabs on him again and to inform me if he enters New Jersey or works his way into my businesses like he has done in the past.

The man has many addictions, and while I promised

his mother on her deathbed I would look out for him, I hadn't anticipated how much a now grown-ass man would need mollycoddled. He's been noticeably absent from our family for almost ten years, preferring to disappear and do whatever the fuck it is he does until he needs money. Truth be told, I've been happy to throw it in his direction just to keep him away from me and my family.

He's a ticking timebomb, and my enemies would love to utilize him to get to me. In all honesty, I would've happily paid them to deal with him had it not been for the niggling feeling of guilt where his mother is concerned.

I don't trust him, not one little bit, and I'm well aware of the extremities people will go to when they have addictions like his. So when he appeared at the Halloween party a couple of years ago looking noticeably cleaner, it only heightened my suspicions. What the hell was he doing coming without even acknowledging any of us? And why, this year, has he once again gone off the radar and not attended?

Odd.

The hairs on the back of my neck stand on end at feeling eyes on me, so I glance around the room and freeze when bright-blue eyes clash with mine, causing my pulse to quicken and my heart to jump start.

It's almost like I can't function, and feeling a lack of control is something I'm not familiar with. It takes a moment for me to regain composure, and when I do, I find myself uncaring if she becomes uncomfortable or conscious of my staring. She's a sight to behold, and if I want to drink her in, I will.

Her long natural-blonde hair has me wanting to wrap it around my fist as I fuck into her, but she's young, too young for someone like me. Knowing everyone here is above legal age, I can allow myself the privilege of soaking up her beauty, but that doesn't mean I should act on my cock thickening at her petite frame and the way her eyes dart away from me when she realizes she's caught my attention.

I've never been a man to take much interest in younger women, preferring the maturity and experience of a woman older than someone bordering on jailbait. However, there's something about her. Something I want to delve into a little more, train maybe.

Her sleek body fits into the tight black leotard like it was specially made for her. A headband with cat ears sits on top of her blonde locks, and a long cat tail trails from her perfectly pert ass. The leotard stretching across her small perky tits exposes her peaked nipples, and my mouth waters to tug them between my teeth and suck until she digs her nails into my scalp, pleading me to stop. The girl is also without makeup, something rare in our community. Only a lick of shimmer on her lips emphasizes how pink they are—innocent, sweet, delectable. Are her pussy lips as pink and perfect? As juicy and ripe?

My balls ache and the tip of my cock rubs against my waistband as I stare at her, devouring her with wild hunger in my eyes.

Her costume and heels elongate her legs, but she's a small thing and delicate-looking too. A perfect little pet for me to dote on and shower with the affection I reserve solely for my pets.

DOMINATION

My body becomes taut at the thought of marking her with my flogger and the way her pale skin will turn red under the palm of my firm hand as I spank her ass and own every inch of her. Then I'll take my time caring for her while she cries her innocence, needing me to comfort and care for her when nobody else can. I'll piece her back together bit by beautiful bit.

Her cheeks pinken while I assess her, her eyes looking everywhere but at me, but she knows she's caught my attention; she can sense me as much as I can her. The heat travels down her body, and I smile and lick my lips like a predator stalking its vulnerable prey.

How pretty she would look with a collar around her delicate neck, letting me control her. Hmm, my little pet would love for me to dominate her with my rough hand.

I want her.

At the realization, my heart thuds against my chest like a drum.

And like that, I decide she's mine.

The tip of my thick cock leaks against my belt, so I shift from side to side to ease the discomfort.

"Should I see if there's been an update on his whereabouts?" Massio asks, and I respond with only a nod because this beauty has captured me in her aura. She's summoned life inside this old man's veins, and I want nothing more than to kiss her delicate lips while holding her chin between my fingers and forcing her attention firmly on me.

"Have a contract drawn up," I rasp.

Massio rears back, eyes widening. He probably thinks I'm going insane, and he'd be right. I never entrap the younger generation, but this one, this one has entrapped me.

"A contract?" He frowns, his eyes ping-ponging over my face.

Reluctantly, I give him my attention, hating that he's distracting me from her. "Yes. A contract." I tilt my head toward the girl, and Massio's eyes follow my action.

He chokes, then clears his throat. "A little young for your usual taste, sir?" If it was anyone else, I would blow a hole between his eyes for questioning me, but because it's Massio, I ignore it. After all, I have known him for years. Hell, his father was one of my capos before his unfortunate demise.

I raise my eyebrow at him, and he shrinks back, then clears his throat. "I'll have one waiting for you in your office within the hour."

"Very well." I gift him a curt nod.

Now Daddy needs to capture his new pet.

And collar her.

Gracie

My blush deepens at his attention on me. The man knows how to command a room, and in the span of an hour, he's managed to command me too.

He's gorgeous, like a *GQ* model. My stomach swirls with excitement and apprehension. The way I'm dressed is provocative and daring, completely unlike me. In fact, this whole event is something I'm uncomfortable with, but I do it anyway because of my family's status. It feels good to be out of the house and away from his control, so with my freedom in sight, I'm determined to see this through.

My cheeks glow at his perusal of my body like he's devouring me, and a ripple of exhilaration courses through me. I try to remain calm, hoping he can't see me for who I am—a girl with zero confidence despite what I'm attempting to portray to the world. I was raised sheltered, away from the outside world by my single mother, and being here on display for the world to see, I feel exposed, a fraud.

He straightens his shoulders, and the man he was speaking to steps back, so I quickly avert my gaze and stare at the empty champagne flute in my hand. The one I threw back to gain some courage to remain here.

Glancing up, I startle when my eyes clash with the man vying for my attention—Vincent Marino, Mafia don of the Marino Family. His feet are a hairsbreadth from mine when he stops toe to toe with me, giving me no choice but to step back. The heady, masculine scent of his cologne causes me to sway on my feet, so his hand grips my arm to steady me. His scent is intoxicating, like his scrutiny, and somehow, his dark eyes become impossibly darker, then his lip twitches in clear amusement that makes my blush deepen further.

"Tsk tsk, Little Pet. Did you have too much to drink already?" He takes the champagne flute from my hand, my jaw falling slack, and I blink at him in shock. Did he just touch me? And did he just call me little pet?

My body heats from the inside out, and when I attempt to pull my arm from his grip, he grasps harder, uncaring if he's leaving bruises on my skin. His jaw tics and his gaze sharpens. "Answer me," he snaps, shaking my arm hard enough my body rocks with the force.

"N-noo."

"No, what?" he grits through clenched teeth.

"N-no, sir. I didn't have too much to drink. I only had the one."

His bunched shoulders relax, his grip loosens, and all signs of anger are dispelled in a matter of seconds. "Good girl. I don't want you drunk for what I have planned for you."

DOMINATION

Wetness pools between my legs at his praise, then embarrassment blooms across my face at the unfamiliar sensation. While his words should send warning sirens off inside me, I'm already enthralled by his presence.

The man is pure sex on a stick, and glancing around the room, I realize I'm not the only one to think it.

Nope, every woman in the room has her eyes on this man, the very man whose attention is purely focused on me, and that knowledge sends a flurry of nervousness through me.

He leans toward my ear, and I suck in a sharp breath. "Why don't you come with me somewhere quiet so we can talk? Get to know one another a little better." His husky voice sends a shiver down my spine, and butterflies take flight in the pit of my stomach.

My feet remain planted as he watches me with intrigue, and I shudder when his attention becomes transfixed on my silky locks. He toys with the strands of my hair, soothing me to a point I want to rest my head in his lap while he caresses it, caresses me.

"Say yes," he breathes. "Be my good girl and say yes," he whispers, his tone full of desperation, and he stares at me with something akin to awe.

"Y-yes," I murmur.

Then his spine stiffens, he takes hold of my hand, spins on his heels, and strides through the ballroom, causing his guests to part to either side of the room for us. His white shirt stretches across his broad back, exposing his muscles, and nerves dance through me at the thought of discovering them. His commanding demeanor has everyone's gaze shifting from him to the floor, and I almost revel in the powerhouse that he is, yet I'm too afraid to. So instead, I lower my head and try to keep up with his heavy footfalls.

His hand tightens around mine as he turns the handle on a solid wood door, and I hope he can't hear the rapid thump of my heart against my ribcage.

Oh, sweet Jesus, what am I doing?

Vinny

My little pet is terrified, scared shitless, and I delight in it. Not because I'm a sadist, not always at least, but because I relish the prospect of providing comfort to my startled little pet like never before.

Hell, I don't know who she is or where the hell she came from, but I intend on finding out.

I just need to get her dainty little fingers to sign the contract giving me full advantage to her without any fallout. The last thing I need is more of a spotlight on me. I've had enough recently to last me a lifetime, and given my track record with women, I need them to know my expectations up front so they don't get any ideas of wanting more from me.

The moment I push into my office and flip the lights on, I know my youngest son, Rocco, has been in here. I can smell the little fucker; the sandalwood cologne he uses is a dead giveaway.

Still, I push the thought of my son aside and concentrate on the fact my cock is busting from my pants. I spin her around to face me. "In here, Little Pet." She strides in, feigning confidence, but I don't miss the tremble in her fingertips. In our world, we rely on noticing every action. After all, it could, one day, save your life.

"Why do you call me that?" Her soft voice sounds innocent, intriguing me, and I have to suppress a shudder of my own as I imagine her on her knees begging so sweetly for a taste of my cum.

"Because you're my pet. Tell me, Little Pet, do you normally go into rooms with men you don't know?"

Her bright eyes widen, and she darts her gaze around the room as if only just realizing the vulnerable position she's landed herself in. "I-I don't."

She withers under my scrutiny, and I lick my lips, biting back the chuckle threatening to escape me. My thick fingers find her narrow hips, holding her tightly to prevent her escape.

Then, out of the corner of my eyes, I see the curtain behind me move slightly, so I sniff the air. I'm going to kill him. I grit my teeth at the thought of Rocco fucking his wife in here when there're multiple other rooms he could take her.

Well, let the little fucker be uncomfortable in the presence of my pet. I smirk to myself and amp up my game.

"Are you going to let Daddy play with you?" My smooth voice fills the air.

Her blue eyes flare with arousal, and a startled gasp leaves her edible little lips. A sound I want to bottle up and keep for myself, one I want no one else hearing, and the thought of my son and potentially his wife witnessing it makes me feel murderous inside.

"What sort of play?" she squeaks.

The word "play" should never be on her lips. Ever. The word alone could bring a man to his knees. My balls ache, and I bite into my lower lip to stifle the feral roar demanding to be released.

"Daddy wants to gag these little lips with his leather belt." Her eyes widen, and I rejoice in the fear floating there.

"Put a collar on this soft, delicate neck of yours"—I drag the tip of my finger down her cheek and over her neck and back up—"and he's going to splash his cum all over this pretty little face. Then I'm going to flip you over and use all your tiny holes while you scream out your pleasure."

My palm rests over her heart, which is hammering furiously, and her small nipples become pointed. Fuck me, that narrow throat will be delicious stuffed with my thick cock as she struggles to take all of me. A spurt of pre-cum has me itching to stroke over my throbbing length, but I resist the urge. I'm fifty-fucking-five not fifteen.

"C-collar me?" She sounds like she's ready to run for the door, but she surprises me by remaining rooted to the spot.

"Hm, a leash too." I grin at her maniacally, imagining using the leash to yank her slender neck back while I fuck her ruthlessly from behind. My perfect little pet being used so thoroughly.

"A leash?"

I nod. "Then Daddy is going to take good care of you. What do you say to that, Little Pet?" I caress her silky locks, delighting in the way she leans toward my touch instead of recoiling like the last little pet I owned.

This one is already the perfect submissive and completely unaware of the fact.

"Y-yes," she pants, high on my promise, and it takes everything in me not to act on my words right here and now.

But the last thing I want is for my son to witness her unravel for me. As much as I know he's in love with his wife, Hallie, I'm also aware that he is a much-younger version of myself, and I don't want to have to ruin his good looks to make me feel better.

"Come, let me take you somewhere special." I step back and hold out my hand, leaving the choice up to her now that she knows my desires.

Take it. I will her with my eyes. *Take it and let me dominate every fucking inch of you.*

"Okay," she murmurs.

With excitement thrumming through me like liquid lust, I stride toward the door, and as I push my little pet through it, I turn my head over my shoulder. "Rocco?" I glare at the curtains. "Get this fucking office fumigated, you little shit," I grit out.

"Yes, sir." I can hear the cocky smile in his tone, and any other time, that would rile me further, but not tonight, not with a promise of domination.

Guiding her through the house with her small hand in mine has my blood pumping wildly. When I take the first step, her feet come to a standstill, so I turn to face her. Uncertainty crosses her pretty features, and I give her hand a reassuring squeeze. "Daddy will look after you always, Little Pet," I rasp, and a soft smile plays on her lips, then she nods and follows me up the stairs.

Need bubbles through my veins as I push open the first bedroom I come to, the one I use solely for my pleasure.

An oversized, four-poster bed takes pride of place in the room, and I release her hand to close the door behind us.

When I turn back to face her, she's fidgeting with her hands and biting into her bottom lip, making her appear even younger, more innocent and coyer.

"Would you like a drink?" I ask, and move to the bar to pour myself a glass of scotch.

"N-no, thank you."

My lip tips up at her sweet manners. "Good girl," I praise, loving the way she drags her tongue over her bottom lip and her eyes flare under my approval.

"Can you take off your clothes, or would you like me to do it for you?" I swallow the amber liquid in one go, then swipe my hand over my mouth. It's practically dripping at the corners at how desperate I am for a taste of her.

She rolls her hands in front of her and looks away, so I lean against the bar, watching her skittish movements, and my cock throbs at how utterly mesmerizing she is.

Then she stands taller and straightens her shoulders. "I can do it."

"Good girl, Little Pet," I croon, stalking toward the bed, then resting my ass on the edge. Exhilaration fills me that I get to witness her undressing for me.

Fuck me, my own personal striptease of the most beautiful creature I've ever set eyes on.

My gaze remains locked on her as she slowly slides off her heels, then lowers the zipper at the side of her leotard. She can only be a little over five foot; a dainty little thing that seems even smaller now and well below my six foot two. Something about our height difference causes my balls to throb with an intensive need to possess every fucking inch of her.

When the flimsy fabric gives way, I can't help but gasp. The air is stolen from my lungs at her sleek, naked little body coming into view for me. Perfection, utter perfection.

The leotard falls to the floor, and she kicks it aside, wiggling her painted toes into the plush carpet. My gaze filled with lust, my bloodstream pumps with wild desire, and I have one thought in mind: I'm going to destroy her.

My fingers fumble with the buttons of my shirt when she looks at me from beneath her thick lashes.

"I'm going to eat your pussy so good, Little Pet. Then Daddy's going to fill your little cunt up with his warm cum." Her lips part, and a whoosh of air leaves her mouth, which only makes my cock grow unbearably harder, the ache in my balls almost too much to handle.

Her pussy is bare, and my cock jumps, eager to glide into her slick folds and force her to stretch to accommodate me. She turns her head away from me, using her hair to conceal her pretty face, and I hate it, but I understand. She's young, inexperienced, and needs her daddy to take control and care for her.

I shrug off my shirt, exposing my toned chest. "Come." I hold out my hand for her, and when she slips hers into mine, I feel like I'm holding the whole universe in the palm of my hand, bringing with it an odd feeling of comfort and security. Something my life has never allowed until this moment.

Something inside me swells, a new realm of power and ownership I've never delved into before now. This little pet is unique compared to all the others, and for the first time in my life, I will our relationship to be just that.

Gracie

The man is the epitome of handsome, domineering, and control. He's everything rolled into one, a silver fox with olive skin and dark-gray eyes bordering on black that consume me with every breath I take.

My body calls to him, and I feel things inside myself I've never felt before now—desire, need, protection. The selfish part of me wants it all, everything he's prepared to give. I'm greedy for his touch, hungry for his words, and desperate for his cravings.

The darkness behind his eyes is carefully constructed, allowing people to only see what he wants them to see, but with the desperation building inside me, I want more. I want to see all of him, every part of him— the tender and the twisted. I know they go hand in hand with a man like him. You're unable to have one without the other.

"Come." He holds his hand out toward me, and my fingers itch to explore his skin. The man can't be much over fifty, yet he's chiseled in a way I've only read about in books. He has ridges and grooves of muscles and a deep V that travels beneath his pants, and ... holy hell, the bulge is huge, and suddenly, I become acutely aware that he might not fit inside me.

"It's okay, Little Pet," he coos, lifting me effortlessly into his lap, then he shuffles us up the bed, and I squeal. "Daddy's going be so gentle with you," he whispers, as if hearing my thoughts. His fingers thread through my hair with tenderness, and I melt into his touch. I seek it out like a beacon of hope, a desperate, needy one. "You're such a pretty girl." I blush at his words. "So beautiful you make Daddy hard." *Oh, dear god.*

"Now, I want to taste your little pussy. Okay?" His question stuns me, and he lifts a brow, awaiting a response, and all I can do is nod, completely intoxicated at the power radiating from him. I'd do anything for his touch in this moment. Anything.

He rests his head back against the pillow, then lifts me to straddle his face, and my lungs seize up with the way his breath whispers over my bare pussy. Looking into his darkened eyes, I'm forced to close my eyes to try and regulate the way my heart ramps up at the feral gleam in his.

When I finally snap my eyes open, my blush deepens. I've never been so close to someone so intimately before now.

My knees straddle either side of his head, and I long to run my fingers through his hair. Instead, I remain motionless, stunned, and his lust-filled eyes hold me captive.

His fingertips pinch into the cheeks of my ass. "Rock

your desperate little cunt over my face, Little Pet. Let me taste your sweet pussy on my tongue."

My breaths become labored as I lower myself against his open mouth.

Am I really doing this?

The first swipe of his tongue is followed with a deep inhale, and he closes his eyes like he's committing my scent to memory. A shiver of delight washes over me at the thought, and I find myself grinding on the scruff of his cropped beard, relishing the way his facial hair prickles my inner thighs. "Oh. Oh, god," I pant, and his eyes flare open. His fingers clench my thighs, bruising my tender skin, and he rocks me back and forth over his face while he laps at my pussy. From my hole to my clit, his tongue works me over, gliding through the juices that escape me. The low vibrations of his ministrations have me panting with need, begging for him to take things further, but his delectable tongue never lingers long enough over my clit. He's holding back, I can feel it, but as much as he attempts to keep me eager, begging, and wanton, I can't help but turn into someone else. I'm no longer the shy, innocent girl the world knows me to be. I've been replaced by a greedy little pet who's eager for her orgasm and desperate for his cock.

"Please," I beg, my tone full of need, and he chuckles against my thighs. "Please, I need it." He sucks at my slick folds and shakes his head from side to side, so I grip the wooden headboard and push down harder against his face, grinding on him. With ecstasy sizzling inside me, arousal leaks from me with each movement he makes, and I revel in the sound of his feral grunts as he devours me.

My pussy clenches, my spine snaps straight, and I throw my head back in sheer euphoria. My orgasm rips through me, shocking me to my very core. Something so intense I scream into the room; my voice ricochets off the walls, and a whimper of satisfaction bubbles up inside me as I slowly come down from the most erotic experience of my entire life.

Vinny

I've never seen anything so spectacular in my entire life. She's simply sensational. I continue to assault her little pussy with my tongue, lapping at her cum as it gushes from her hole in lavish waves. I plunge my tongue inside her, and her ass thrusts harder against me, begging to be filled.

Her chest rises, and she continues to ride out the pleasure taking over her small body, and I bask in it. The head of my cock is peeking out of my pants, bulging against my belt and causing a bite of pain I choose to ignore. She's unaware of my predicament, the way my cock is eager to get in on the action, and the need to thrust inside her while she clings to me for sanctuary becomes unbearable. Her head is tipped back, and the ends of her hair brush my abs, each movement causing me to hiss. I struggle to rein in my need to slam inside and destroy her little body in the best ways possible.

Without warning her, I flip her into position, throwing her onto the mattress so hard she bounces with a giggle. I make quick work of unbuckling my belt while she chews on her bottom lip, watching me with splendor.

A man of my age has no place sliding between the slim silky thighs of a girl young enough to be my daughter, and while I wouldn't normally pursue someone so young, I don't seem to have it in me to care tonight. There's something about her I want, crave even, so I will take it—a carnal need to make her mine, consequences be damned.

Without even taking my pants off, I position the head of my cock at her small opening, every muscle in my body taut with need. My cock leaks copious amounts of pre-cum over my hand as I push the swollen tip of my cock into her warm heat, stretching her hole to capacity.

My eyebrows pinch together as I edge inside her. The way her body resists me shouldn't be an aphrodisiac, but it is, because in this moment, I realize my little pet is giving me her virginity. It's written all over her in the way her body tenses, her tight hole contracts with resistance while I continue to slowly force myself inside her, and the way her eyes fill with tears. She turns her head to the side when I sink inside her farther and nudge at her barrier. Fuck, that feels good. So fucking good, knowing I'm the only person to ever have entered her. Her virgin walls grip my cock, and I still above the most beautiful woman I've ever laid eyes on.

"Let me in, Little Pet. Let Daddy fuck your little hole nice and deep." I lean over her and take her chin between my fingers just how I imagined, guiding her to face me. "Let Daddy fill you up." I trail my nose up her face, then lick away the wetness seeping from her eyes. "Let Daddy in, and I'll make you feel good." I grind my hips to relieve the budding ache to thrust. "Do as you're told, and I'll take it easy on this little pussy."

"Oh, god! It won't fit," she cries out when my cock flexes inside her.

"Daddy will make it fit," I croon.

Her breathing stutters, and my little pet gives me a coy nod I so desperately needed.

When my lips breeze over hers, I force my tongue between her lips and surge forward, tearing through her innocence. Her back arches and her fingernails claw at my shoulders, and I swallow down her cry.

A gush of warmth greets me, and I almost come on the spot. Stilling above her, I pull back to survey her blue eyes, but she has them closed. "Look at me!" I demand with a push of my hips. "Look at Daddy while I take your virgin pussy!" I grind out. My gaze travels down to the head of my cock to witness it stretching her little cunt, leaving me no choice but to push inside her another inch. I need to fuck her, really fuck her. Own her little body inside and out.

Then without giving her a chance to consider the pain she's enduring, I snap my hips back and follow it up with another deep slam, taking the air from her lungs and finally filling her to the hilt.

Her pussy is so fucking tight I bite into the side of my cheek to stop myself from spilling inside her.

Then I rear back and watch in sick fascination as her blood, combined with our pleasure, trickles down my cock; it's a spectacular sight. A need to claim her comes over me, a possession so strong I want to dominate her entire being.

My balls draw up, and my cock jumps, then I slam inside her again and again. I pound into her pussy, giving her a grind of my hips on each thrust, hoping I swell her little bud to tenderness once again.

My mouth crashes against hers, and my tongue sweeps through her mouth as I assault her little body, and the thought only makes me harder at how small she is compared to me. How she clings to me has my chest swelling with pride; she's mine.

Sweat beads on my forehead with each feral thrust.

My bloody little pet.

My little pet to protect.

"Fuck, you feel so good!" I grunt. Her small pussy hole throbs against my cock with each intrusion, and the feeling is fucking incredible.

My cock becomes painful, and I close my eyes, giving myself over to her and thrusting forward one final time before stilling to fill her with my cum. Rope after fucking rope of hot cum fills her little cunt until it runs down my balls, along with the red streak of her innocence that has my cock jumping with a need to satiate once again.

When I pull back to stare into her teary blue eyes, my breathing quickens, and she holds my heart captive as I steady my pace. I slowly rock back and forth, and my cock twitches back to life. "There, there, Little Pet. Let Daddy make you feel good now that you're a big girl." I press my lips to hers, and she wraps her arms around my neck, so I allow her to take the lead. With one hand above her head, I kiss over her jaw and down her neck, breathing in her scent, then I pepper her small tit with soft kisses. Her hips buck beneath me when I circle her nipple with my tongue, and I relish the way her pussy grips me as I toy with it. Moving my free hand between us, I circle her clit in time with my tongue.

"Oh. Oh, please."

I crook an eyebrow at her.

"Daddy. Daddy, please," she pants wantonly.

My eyes glow with satisfaction, and I press down on her clit while sucking her nipple to a pointed bud. "Hmm," I groan when her pussy muscles squeeze me like a goddamn vise. "Fuck. That's it, squeeze Daddy's thick cock, little girl."

"Yes. Yes. I'm ..." She arches her back, and her orgasm hits her, causing me to grunt in approval. A roar of satisfaction rips from deep inside me, and my cock floods her pussy with my hot cum, marking her as mine once again.

With my body aching, I roll onto my side to pull my little pet toward me, but when I open my arm, it's met with a cold pillow. My eyes flare open and find the bed empty, void of her presence.

What the fuck?

Irritation builds in my chest, so I throw off the sheets and head toward the bathroom. Nothing. Then I storm back into the bedroom, swipe my pants off the floor, and shove my feet into them before buttoning them and heading toward the door with fury running through my veins.

I should have chained her to the fucking bed like I usually do, but I let the fact she's innocent take over my brain. Unlike myself, I allowed her a small part of control, and now it's biting me in the ass.

After fucking her a dozen times into oblivion, I crashed beside her, spent for the night.

"Massio!" I bark, and meet him halfway down the stairs.

"Sir?" His eyes widen, no doubt a reflection of my frantic state.

"The girl from my bed. Did she sign the contract?" His eyes ping-pong over my face, and I feel myself becoming pissed. "Well?!" I bellow, causing him to jolt.

He swallows, and even the time he takes to do that aggravates me further. "I put it in the office like you asked."

My chest rises and falls—she never signed the contract. She never signed it because my fucking son was using my office in some sort of roleplay scenario with his wife who was once his teacher. The way she was dressed for the party tells me they were reenacting a scene, and I wince that my mind went there.

"She didn't sign it," I state, my voice solemn as I push a hand through my hair.

"Do you want me to track her down?" Massio eyes me skeptically.

Do I?

I want her, badly. But the girl was young, very young, too young for me.

She will want things; things I can't give her. All I

want from her is her compliance and her delectable body at my beck and call as my submissive, my pet.

Do I do it? Tell him to track her down and selfishly take what I want, or do I let her go to be the free spirit she clearly wants to be.

"Sir?"

A lump gathers in my throat, and I contemplate my options.

I can't give women what they want, I never could and never will, and with as much as I marked that girl last night, she marked me more. For the first time in my life, the girl is more than just a pet.

She is mine, and I want her to be.

I claimed her.

"Leave it," I grunt out, and turn my back, heading up the stairs, already regretting my decision. When I enter the bedroom and her peach scent encompasses me, it only cements it.

The sheets are marked with the perfect blend of our combined juices, her innocence, and my domination.

She was meant to be mine, and I let her go. With my head resting on the door, I remind myself I may be a bad man, but there's still some good in me. I just proved that, if only to myself.

Being bad doesn't have to be your entirety.

In a world of darkness, you can be someone's light and lead them to a better life.

That's what I will tell myself to get over her absence.

I set her free when I could have caged her.

Chapter One

Vinny

Eighteen months later ...

Annoyance pounds inside my chest at the spiel coming from my stepson's mouth. My oldest son, Rafael, rolls his eyes in my direction, and I pull my lips into a tight line to refrain from smirking.

"I've tried, Vinny. I swear. I just need a little help," he drones on. "This time is different." Of course it fucking is. Like the last time ... and the time before that.

Rafael shifts in his chair, so I know he's becoming agitated. My son has zero patience where Robert is concerned, but I refuse to cut him off. His mother, Nancy, was a good woman, and it was her dying wish for me to look out for him despite knowing he was a lost cause.

Rafael sits forward, and his gaze slices toward Robert. "How much?"

"Wh-what do you mean?" Robert splutters.

"How much money do you want from my father this time? My family." Rafael's voice is deadly, causing the hairs on the back of my neck to stand on end, and I couldn't be prouder.

Using my finger, I stroke my bottom lip and sit back in my chair, watching this play out.

"I-it's not like that." Robert's eyes implore me. "This time I want it to work. I need it to work." His hands ball into fists on his lap.

"What's so different this time, Robert?" I say deadpan, trying to keep the amusement from my tone.

"My daughter, Gracie. She has a little girl." He gulps.

Rafael rears back, but I don't give away my emotion so easily, masking the shock of my stepson having a granddaughter.

How was I not made aware of this?

"She-she's dependent on me. They both are, and I need to be the best man I can for them." He holds eye contact, but I narrow my eyes, then he looks away, unable to hold the intensity of my glower. Sly little fucker.

I hadn't realized Robert's daughter was old enough to have a child. Jesus, how old does that make me? I drag my hand through my hair, and the coarse tips of the silver between my fingers is so unlike the silky locks of my lost little pet.

Rafael shifts in his chair, bringing my attention back to the here and now. My son has been desperate to take over for a while now, and though he's capable, I just don't want the responsibility resting completely on him and his young family. Besides, there's plenty of life left in me yet.

"My granddaughter deserves the best in life," he states.

Does that make me the kid's great-grandfather? Fuck! Another responsibility.

"Where's the fucking father to this child?" Rafael bites out, and I know his mind is solely on Robert trying to push someone else's responsibility onto us.

But we are, after all, this girl's family.

"H-he's a loser. Gracie met him at church." Church? Rafael releases a patronizing chuckle, and I can't fault him. Fucking church, of all places.

Robert probably steals from the congregation while claiming his repentance.

"Pl-please." He chokes on his tears and swipes at the snot dripping from his nose as his body shakes.

Good fucking god, the man is a wreck. I want to tell him to stop blubbering and sit up straight, to face me like a real man, but it's clear he's having withdrawals, and he's desperate, very fucking desperate. He sits up straighter. "I-I told him if he couldn't man up, then I would. He's not been around since." His spine goes ramrod straight, and his tears clear like he's suddenly a new person, one proud of his words.

"So *you* manned up?" Rafael drawls, and I stifle my smile at my son's sarcasm.

"I did." Robert lifts his chin.

"Poor fucking girl," Rafael mumbles.

I steeple my fingers on the desk in front of me. "So, what exactly do you need from me?"

The sly little fucker smiles, then swiftly masks it, but being brought up in the Mafia, I've learned the common traits and tactics people use without always realizing. The giveaways become like second nature to us. Rafael meets my eyes, and I know he saw it too.

"Well, there's this rehab facility in Washington."

He opens his mouth to continue, but I hold my hand up to stop him. "No. Any rchab facility will be chosen by us this time." We've become accustomed to Robert's idea of a rehab facility, and frankly, it's nothing more than a bunch of money-hungry pricks who allow their patients to run amuck. They're mostly funded by mommy and daddy, so the rich little fuckers don't even feel the pinch of their own fuckups.

He nods his head, giving in far too quickly for my liking. "I was hoping my daughter and granddaughter could stay here. I don't trust that fucker around her and the baby."

Rafael's and my body tense. "Is he going to be an issue?" I ask, needing to be made aware of any potential threats.

"N-no." He shakes his head furiously. "Just keep him away from her. She's a good girl, and she's lost her way since ... him," he grits out.

"If the baby is his ..." Rafael asserts.

"It is," he bites back. "But he's not a good role model for either of them."

This coming from the man who has spent most of his daughter's life being an absent parent and only stepping up when he had no choice and her mother passed away. I might not have had much contact with Robert over recent years, but I made sure I had tabs on him. I just hadn't realized how old his daughter actually is, and he's made it a mission to avoid our family invitations unless it suits him.

"He takes drugs, deals them. I know he's been stealing credit cards from other churchgoers, praying on their good nature." He sounds like he's describing himself, and I have to stifle the smile that threatens to break free. "That's why I kept her home during the pregnancy. I don't want my daughter around someone like that."

It's on the tip of my tongue to tell him he doesn't want someone like himself around his daughter, but Rafael opens his mouth, so I quickly shake my head, and he snaps it shut. I know damn well my son was about to say exactly what I was thinking.

My finger toys with my bottom lip as I contemplate my next move. Robert appears genuine, but he always has. However, now he has a daughter and granddaughter in his care, something to get clean for, and Nancy would have been devastated if I'd turned away her flesh and blood, her granddaughter and great-grandchild, no less. They, at least, deserve more.

Jesus, I'm fucking old.

Taking a deep breath, I hope I don't regret what I'm about to do. "They can stay."

Rafael jolts, but Robert sits taller. The smile on his lips is cunning and not one I'm fond of. It's not lost on me there's not a single hair on his head that I like, I only hope his daughter is different.

Chapter Two

Gracie

"Remember your manners, and don't let the kid run wild."

I bite into my cheek to stop myself from responding. My father doesn't so much as speak Bonnie's name, and run wild? She doesn't even walk yet, and remember my manners? Since when don't I remember my manners? My mother brought me up the right way; she was everything pure and genuine in the world, but my father? He's the complete opposite.

When I was fourteen, she passed away from cancer, and the day my father came to collect me from the only home I'd ever known was soul destroying. I'd only met the man once before, and that was when he came to the ranch I grew up on, demanding money or custody of me. My mom complied, and I didn't see him again until the day after her funeral when he came to take me to live with him. He's spent every day since reminding me of his sacrifice for me. According to him, he could be at the heart of a privileged family by now, but they wanted nothing to do with me because I was born out of wedlock. Instead, my father drowned his sorrows in alcohol and indulged in drugs. He spent months away from the house he owned, and I was only too grateful for that. When my father was home, he was not a nice person to be around. I preferred my solitude to dream about my future, one without him in it.

My mom said when she met him, he was a different man, before the addictions took over, and I can only live in hope that one day he becomes that man again. For now, I'm grateful because his extended family has offered me and my daughter sanctuary while my father is away hopefully becoming a better person, and even more, I'm hoping to use this time to get out from under his clutches once and for all. While I wish my father well for his future, I want him to stay the hell out of mine, and more importantly, I want to go home.

Vinny

There's a knock at the dining room door, and it's followed by Massio's face. "Sir, your guests have arrived."

"Show them in." I wave a nonchalant hand in the air.

He gives me a curt nod, then disappears, and moments later, the sound of a gasp draws my attention to the doorway.

Massio guides the stunned girl into the room while my heart races wildly in my chest.

Massio clears his throat. "This is Gracie, sir. Your … your step-granddaughter." He winces, probably unsure he should be saying it at all.

A bolt of pain hits me in the chest, but I mask the grimace threatening to release from me at the sight of the girl before me.

My lost little pet. Now, it seems, found.

Excitement zips through me at lightning speed, and my cock hardens. She's here. In my home.

She returned.

Despite the circumstances surrounding her, I know one thing for sure: I'm chaining her to me. Literally.

"And her daughter." Massio nods toward the little bundle in her arms, and my chest constricts. The little girl has her mother's blonde hair, but it's curly at the tips unlike her mother's straight head of hair. There's a small pink bow clasped at the side of her head, and she turns her face toward mine, causing my heart to still at the little blue eyes, like her mother's, shining back at me. She's a mirror image of her and utterly adorable.

A fierce, possessiveness rushes through me as my temple pulsates with growing aggravation. Some fucker slept with her and gave her this beautiful gift of life. The tension in my temple escalates along with my temper. She fucked me, then fucked another man so soon after while I've been left struggling to get over her.

Did she use me to get rid of her virginity?

Did she want some experience to use with another?

I thought she was different but have been proved otherwise by her actions, then a sudden deep-seated hatred runs through my veins.

My hand tightens around my scotch, and I struggle to remain calm in the wake of her presence.

She wears a blue sundress that brings out the shade of her eyes, and has a pair of flip-flops on her feet.

"Don't just stand in the doorway, Gracie, for Christ's sake. Sit!" her father booms, and she jumps, then the baby's bottom lip wobbles. She caresses the baby's back in a soothing motion, and almost instantly, the movement relaxes me too. She's a good mom.

Gracie moves toward the seat farthest from me, and

my jaw tics. She slowly lowers herself as though the seat will hurt her ass.

"Your grandfather doesn't fucking bite. Sit there!" I grimace at Robert's title for me, but I'm thrilled when he points to the chair next to me. I have and never will be this girl's grandfather, but I sure as shit can be her daddy. My lips tip up into a sly smirk as I imagine making her pay for betraying me.

If she wants to act like a whore, then I intend to treat her like one.

My gaze roams over her, and she lifts her head from her daughter to face her father. He pulls out the chair beside me, so she stands and moves toward him, and keeping her eyes on the table, she slowly takes the seat.

Having him in my proximity is not at the top of my list, and I cluck my tongue at the irritation his presence brings, but I remain transfixed on her.

The obvious glare of contempt I'm throwing her way doesn't go unnoticed. In fact, the blush sweeping over her cheeks and down her bare chest is somewhat telling, and the slight hitch in her breathing gives away her discomfort at my scrutiny, and she should be uncomfortable. I might have missed out on her becoming my little pet last time, but I won't this time. I'll make sure of it.

"Gracie has been looking forward to staying with you and getting to know the family, isn't that right, Gracie?" Robert prompts, and I lift my eyebrow, waiting for her to reply.

She swallows hard before glaring back at me head-on. "Yes."

"Is that so?"

She tosses her hair over her shoulders and sits straighter, feigning confidence. "Yes. Very much."

"And your daughter, is she excited to be here too?" I watch her, my eyes drilling into hers.

"*Bonnie* is a baby. I'm sure you're aware she doesn't understand what we're doing here." Anger flares in her eyes as she snipes back at me, and I release a low chuckle at her fire that before now had been absent.

"Gracie!" Robert booms, then she flinches, and little Bonnie whimpers in her mother's arms, making my hand clench into a fist. "Enough! Before you ruin things for me like you ruin everything else," he snipes.

The way the man speaks leads me to believe the girls are used to this, and if there's anything I don't like, it's assholes being abusive toward women. They're nothing more than cowards. Something I've taught all four of my sons not to be nor to stand for.

"Keep your fucking voice down, and don't speak to them that way," I grit out through clenched teeth. He opens his mouth to speak, but when I slice my gaze toward him, he snaps his mouth shut, gulping, and I almost want to chuckle at his compliance. *Fucking coward.*

"Sir, would you like dinner to be served?" Hazel, my head housekeeper, asks.

"Yes, thank you."

She nods in my direction, then leaves the room.

Staring at my new pet, I zone out of whatever bullshit Robert is filling me in on about stocks and shares at his company and how excited he is to return to his job after rehab to take on new investments I might be interested in. The man is deluded if he thinks I'm remotely interested in working with him. Other than his daughter, of course.

Ignoring Robert, I tilt my head and watch the way Gracie cares for little Bonnie; she cuts her vegetables from her plate, then hand feeds them to her while somehow holding her hand beneath her chin to collect the mess.

"She knows better than to let her drop shit on the floor." Robert points his fork toward the girls, and I stiffen. "I've told her to make sure she doesn't cause you any problems, you won't know you've got them, I can assure you of that," he says with a deep sneer.

The way he speaks has my bloodstream filling with so much anger it sizzles through me, boiling beneath my skin, so I clench my teeth. Exhaling my anger, I shake off his words, opting to comfort Gracie.

I clear my throat. "Gracie, I'd like you to make a list of anything you need ordered for Bonnie."

She pushes her hair behind her ear, and I realize she's been using it as a curtain to shut both me and her father out, and I hate it. So much so I wonder if it's necessary to keep it so long, until I remember the silky feel of it between my fingers and the way it grazed over my abs and balls when she threw her head back in ecstasy. It's necessary.

"Thank you, but we won't need anything." She turns her attention back to her meal and daughter, and annoyance rumbles in my chest. I want to care for them, and she has no choice but to let me.

If I want to shower them with gifts, I will.

Robert interjects while waving a hand in their direction. "See. They won't be an issue. You won't even know you've got them."

Somehow, I very much doubt that.

Chapter Three

Gracie

The moment our eyes connected, I wanted to run and never look back, but I can't. Not yet anyway. My heart hammered precariously and my mind whirled a mile a minute with the incredible memories of one night over a year ago.

His white shirt was open at the chest, and I longed to stroke his olive skin, kiss and caress it while he played with my hair.

The way his sleeves are rolled up to his elbows, exposing his bronzed arms, reminds me of the night he changed my destiny.

I shake my head. *Keep your head on straight, Gracie.*

As I've spent so long confined by my father's rules, I intend to use staying here to my advantage. My agreement to come here was nothing short of strategic, and with that thought in mind, I swallow back the nervousness bubbling up my throat and threatening to erupt at any given moment.

While my father and Vinny conversed during dinner, I spent my time caring for my daughter. Bonnie is almost ten months now and an absolute delight. She's my reason for living, the light in the darkest of days, and I want nothing more than to give her the freedom I had when growing up. Before it all went to hell.

When my father turns his attention toward me, I try not to cower at his cruel words. Thankfully, Vinny doesn't seem remotely like my father, but he's told me enough times how bad the Marino family is, so I want to reserve judgment on them. I also want to make sure I don't fall into his bed again. The last time was almost enough to destroy me, and I refuse to let that happen.

"You can order her a new chair, perhaps? One of those baby ones." Vinny waves his hand in my direction, and I slink back, wishing I could just order items for her when I need them. I'm well aware of the many items my daughter is missing out on, but when I return home to my mother's ranch, I can build her a better life there, away from any threats of violence or promises of taking my child from me.

"No, thank you. We're fine."

"See, I told you they don't need anything," my father singsongs.

Vinny pushes back in his chair, and it screeches against the wooden floor. I recoil when Robert glares in my direction, but Vinny stalks past the table to the door and calls his housekeeper in. Then she rushes into the room just as his ass touches the seat again.

"Hazel. Could you please show Gracie and little Bonnie to their room while I show Robert out." The housekeeper nods, and my eyes widen at his stern tone and the way he's practically banishing us all. We haven't even finished dinner. "And send them snacks up to their room, please."

"Of course, sir. This way, miss." The housekeeper's warm smile greets me. Her hair is in a messy bun, littered with silver streaks, and she has pretty green eyes that shimmer with warmth, so I find myself relaxing for the first time since leaving my father's home.

"Come on, sweetie." I gather Bonnie into my arms to stand and take one last glance in Vinny's direction, and the promising glint in his eyes has trepidation rippling through my bloodstream. Something tells me he's far from done with me, and the rush of anticipation is an emotion I have no place feeling.

Hazel is kind and has a gentle tone about her as she shows me around. I pick up on an Italian accent, and I wonder how Vinny sounds when he speaks in Italian. My cheeks flush at the thought, and I quickly turn away from Hazel before she can witness it.

The white furnishings appear new, and there's a scattering of pink around the room that makes me wonder if she had a hand in decorating. "I chose the pink," she confirms with a proud smile. "We don't have any girls in the immediate family. So this makes me very happy." She smiles toward Bonnie, and my heart soars at the affection emanating from her. "Sir has four strapping boys." My lip quirks at her reference to them being boys when they are very much men, which I know, thanks to my father's avid jealousy.

The soft carpet has my toes curling into the pile; the room is simply beautiful. A glass chandelier hangs from the ceiling, and a white wooden bed sits proudly in the center of the room. It has small flowers carved into the headboard, and the white bedding with pink pillows and matching blankets are laid perfectly on top.

"This here is little Bonnie's nursery." Hazel opens a door, and when I poke my head inside, I gasp, and my eyes fill with tears. It's everything I ever dreamed of for her, more even. Something catches in my chest, and I force myself to exhale through the emotion.

"I hope you're both going to be very happy here, Miss Gracie." Hazel pats my arm.

Emotion lodges in my throat, and I choke on my words. "Please just call me Gracie."

"Yes, miss," she says, and I can't help but to smile. "I'll leave you to explore."

"Thank you."

When she turns to walk away, my feet bring me into the nursery on their own accord, and it's truly a room fit for a little princess. "Look, Bonnie, you're such a lucky girl." Bonnie makes grabby hands toward the chest of soft toys on the floor, so I place her down. She makes a beeline for them, crawling toward the chest, and I giggle as she throws the soft toys while making content sounds that have my heart swelling.

A white crib sits against the wall, and I trace the

floral design etched into the wood that matches my bed. Again, white crib sheets and a fluffy pink blanket lay at the base, and I can't help but run my hand over the soft fabric. So unlike the rough, scratchy sheets at home.

"We need to talk." His gruff voice has me spinning on the balls of my feet to face him, and his temple pulsates. He has a tic in his jaw and glares at me with blazing eyes and flaring nostrils. I hate being the reason for his anger.

My fingers tremble as I tuck my hair behind my ear, and I swallow back the lump in my throat, nodding.

He stretches his arm out toward my room, and I glance at Bonnie, who is unaware of the tension building between Vinny and me. Instead, she's shoving soft toys in her mouth while cooing.

"She will be fine in here, and we'll leave the door open," Vinny adds, causing a slither of apprehension to slip from me.

Dread lines my stomach, and I take a deep breath. I don't like that he's witnessing how nervous I am, but it's not like I can hide it, the man unravels me in a way that's completely foreign to me.

I want to make him proud, I want him to shower me with praise and look at me with longing, like I'm his entire world. If only for the night again.

The moment I step into the bedroom and move to walk past him, he grips my arm and spins me to face him. His touch scorches my skin, and I melt, my body becoming like putty as I stare into his stormy-gray eyes that are darkening by the second.

"Did you know?" he asks, and my lips part to speak,

but nothing comes out. He shakes me. "Did you know?" he booms, causing me to flinch, and his body goes lax.

His free hand slowly rises to my face, and my breath stutters, then he tucks a lock of my hair behind my ear. "Did you know your father was my stepson?"

The smell of his cologne filters through my nostrils. The way I could still smell him on my skin after our night together has been engrained in my mind. His proximity has clouded my mind and made my throat dry. "N-no."

I clear my throat, hoping I can sound more confident this time. "No, I didn't know." His eyes scan my face, then he nods and releases my arm, and already, I wish he hadn't. Although I don't know why, I feel safe when I'm with him, and it's a feeling I've longed for since our night together.

He takes a step back, but his focus remains on me, and I follow the way his Adam's apple slides down his throat. The top two buttons on his white dress shirt are open, exposing his olive skin that I long to graze with my fingernail and kiss and lick and ...

"I want you to sign this contract." He holds up a bunch of papers, and my eyes narrow. Is it an NDA? If so, it's unnecessary. I won't tell anyone a damn thing. I just want to be left alone, to live my life away from anyone and any threat, and be safe and happy.

"Now, be a good girl and sign it." He shoves the papers into my chest, causing me to stumble. "I expect them in my office before you go to bed tonight."

Tears fill my eyes at his abrupt tone; he's shutting me out once again. He's barely even acknowledged our night together, and now he's dismissing me like it meant nothing.

As the door clicks shut behind him, I gape down at the papers in my hand and follow the text slowly.

Contract between: Vincent Marino (Daddy) and Gracie Ramsey (Little Pet).

What the hell?

Chapter Four

Gracie

My eyes widen even more the further I read on: *Little Pet will remain submissive while her collar is on. Should she not behave, Little Pet will be punished accordingly. Collar is not to be removed by anyone but Daddy.*

Punished? Collar? My body heats as I remember when he told me he wanted to collar me, but I never took the threat seriously.

Does he do this a lot? Collar women? Take them as his pets?

Jealousy creeps up my spine, and I shudder at the fact he could have pets living in the mansion now?

Does he have lots of women? Pets?

I skip down a few paragraphs, rubbing my eyes: *Little Pet will give Daddy full control of her body, therefore no touching her private regions without prior consent.* Just who the hell does he think he is? Prior consent. My blood boils, but something other than anger is simmering inside me; maybe intrigue too? To have someone as powerful and caring control my body for me sounds liberating. Someone who cares for my needs when I've spent so long caring for myself. Submitting to him would almost feel freeing. He could think on my behalf, and all I'll have to do is comply. Pushing the thought aside, I shake my head, refusing to be drawn in no matter how inviting the idea is. I need to stay on task. Do what I need to do so I can return home.

I flip through the countless pages, trying my best to concentrate on the words.

Little Pet must discuss in advance any activities she is not comfortable with, and those will not be pursued. A safe word of 'Red' will be used when Little Pet is not comfortable, and all forms of play will be immediately halted.

I skim over the activities: *edging, spanking, role play, anal play, bondage, gags, suspension, voyeurism, fisting.* Oh, god. My cheeks flush and my heart races. I can't do those things. I can't. The list goes on and on. While I've heard of most of these things, I've never heard of *watersports.*

Just what the hell is a watersport, and why is it mentioned as something you would do in a bedroom?

He wants me to become his pet? I glance toward the door. He can't be serious. He just found out I'm his step-granddaughter. Is that a thing?

Bonnie pulls me out of my thoughts when she whimpers in the nursery. It's getting to be time for her feeding.

DOMINATION

Afterward, I'll bathe her in the spacious bathroom, then put her to bed and turn on the baby monitor in her nursery so I can go and discuss this contract with the man who consumes my thoughts and, it appears, my body too.

Chapter Five

Vinny

"What the hell do you mean we're being searched again?" I shout.

"Yes, again!" Rafael bellows, his vicious tone mirroring my own.

My three sons fill the office, all eyes on me as Rafael recalls what went down during the early hours of this morning.

We've always been on the police commissioner's radar—Harrison Davis—but since my son took his ex-daughter-in-law as a wife, it's gotten increasingly worse. Coupled with the fact that Rocco played a part in his son's death, the man is out for retribution. I've had no choice but to utilize the support of the O'Connell Mafia to keep our shipments coming in.

Thankfully, they have connections with a different MC than the one my absent son is linked to, and they're willing to distribute our firearms and take the fall at a cost, if need be. Between time, I'm trying to maintain our legal businesses while dodging the fucking set ups at the same time.

Last week, the manager of one of our strip clubs was hauled into the precinct for supposedly distributing drugs. Turns out, he had no part in it and didn't even recognize the culprit. He knows to keep squeaky clean at the minute. We can't risk any more attention on us than usual.

Pushing my fingers through my hair, I pin my glare on my son Tommy. During one point in his life, he lost his way. It took his stepdaughter staying with him to realize what value he had in life. I'm proud of the man he's become. He's a great husband and a wonderful father to their young children; something I wish I could say for myself. My biggest regret in life is none of my children having a mother figure. Not a single one was fit for the role I'd married them for, and while I think it hardened the boys to the Mafia way of life, I didn't miss the way they craved the softness I was unable to give them over the years.

Maybe that's why I'm so caring in the bedroom, I can finally be myself. Albeit with a contract signed that allows it without the risk of showing vulnerability to the outside world, and should retribution take place, my emotions won't be hindered.

My mind races toward the gift I have upstairs. Two gifts, to be precise. As much as my cock aches to be inside Gracie again, I can't forget her daughter either, so when I finally collar the girl who escaped me for months, I must

DOMINATION

bear in mind the rules may need to be bent slightly to accommodate a baby.

"Can you deal with it?" I snipe out at Rafael, then a sliver of guilt hits me for speaking to him so abruptly.

"Of course," he states, used to my sharp tone.

"Are you ready for bed, old man?" my youngest son, Rocco, taunts. He's almost twenty and is more a man than my thirty-six-year-old stepson will ever be. He stepped up and took what he wanted, which just so happened to be Gerrard Davis's wife and son. Shame I'm now reaping the consequences of his actions. Gerrard, the abusive bastard he was, ended up dead, and now we're left with the aftermath of dealing with his father. Fortunately for us, we know a lot of people, so with each allegation they arrest us for, we knock them back while formulating a long-term plan to take out the real threat once and for all.

"Are you sure you can trust your sources?" Rocco asks, sitting forward. The tattoo creeping up the column of his throat depicting his woman's name makes my lip twitch. Crazy little fucker had it done to mark their one-year anniversary.

"Yes. I'm sure," I say with confidence.

"So, what, we just trust them that Harrison is just going to disappear?" Tommy asks, with skepticism lacing his tone.

My sons are right to be suspicious. When you're in the Mafia, many parts of it are entwined with some of the other five families, and sometimes, all you can do is put your trust in them despite your natural reaction not to.

"I trust them," I say, referring to the Varros family

and the intel they have regarding Harrison. "Owen assures me he has a plan."

Owen Stevens is part owner of STORM Enterprises; he's the head of their security, and those men have their fingers in every Mafia pie. While that should leave me wide open to become vulnerable, it doesn't. I've dealt with Owen plenty of times.

"I trust Owen, and Lorenzo Varros has good reason to hold a grudge too," Rafael confirms. "He did disclose there's another backer on the West Coast that wants rid of Harrison for reasons nobody is prepared to disclose."

That's news to me, but it only shows how deep and far Harrison's treachery has gone. "Any ideas who?"

Rafael cracks his neck from side to side. "Not yet, but I'm sure we will find out soon enough."

"How'd it go with Robert and the kids?" Rocco leans back in his chair, picking at his nails with a knife, looking every bit the maniac he is.

Jesus. I grimace at the thought of him referring to Gracie as a child. My boys have known about my sexual preferences for a long while now. Hell, I should've probably kept them hidden from them over the years, protected them more. Just another fuck-up of mine. I drag a hand through my hair.

What they will be surprised at is the fact I've taken to a girl as young as her.

When Massio gave me her file this afternoon, I wasn't surprised to find she's almost twenty. That made her eighteen when I fucked her. An eighteen-year-old virgin, for fuck's sake.

Well, it appears she moved on and got some experience pretty fast, which pisses me the fuck off, but I intend to show her what a real man is. I'll put her lithe little body to the test until she's dripping in a puddle of my cum.

"Oh, fuck, I know that look." Rocco sits straighter and leans forward. "Papa has a hard-on for the girl."

I roll my eyes while Rafael's eyes drill into me with venom. "You've got to be fucking kidding me? She's too young for you," he splutters, distaste oozing from him.

Rocco's chuckle fills the room while Tommy scans me, no doubt checking I have full use of my faculties. I may have lost my mind, but everything else is in full working order.

Casually, I lift a shoulder. "It appears I want a change."

"Change? She's the same age as my wife!"

"And mine," Tommy adds.

"Don't worry, Papa. She's not the same age as mine." Rocco grins. "I like women, not young girls that don't know how to please a man."

Rafael seethes, his face turning red, narrowing his gaze on Rocco. Jesus, he looks like he's two seconds away from tearing Rocco apart. I need to dispel the onslaught before it happens.

"Maybe that's where we find the fun, Rocco. Teaching our girls how to take cock, knowing nobody's been there before us. Right, Papa?" Tommy counters, and I pinch the bridge of my nose, willing my cock to go down after the thought of Gracie learning to take my girth down her slender throat flashes through my mind.

Rocco scoffs. "I'd rather teach her a lesson for

knowing how to do it in the first place." The gleam in his eyes tells me how sincere his words are, and if it was anyone other than my son talking so inappropriately, I'd probably revel in it. But the fact it's my youngest boy has me blanching.

I slam my hand down on the desk, causing the stationery to jump. "Enough!"

The office falls silent, and as if on cue, a low knock sounds from the door, and I know it's her.

My sons' eyes flick toward me. "Not a fucking word," I warn, not liking the way Rocco's lip curls at the edge.

"Come in!" I bite out, and my adrenaline spikes with her nearness.

Chapter Six

Gracie

"Come in!" he booms, and I jump like a cat on hot bricks. *Jeez, calm down, Gracie, show him he doesn't control you.* I swipe my clammy hands down my dress, pull my shoulders back, lift my chin, then open the door and march into the room. His eyes roam over me, but I ignore them and the way they cause heat to flush over my body. Instead, I keep the task at hand in the forefront of my mind and slam the papers on his desk.

"What the hell are these?" I demand. He opens his mouth to speak, but I hold my palm up. "I am not a pet, nor do I want to be. And a collar? For what possible reason would I want a collar around my neck like a damn noose. And watersports? In the bedroom? Would it not be best to confine it to somewhere more appropriate like a swimming pool? How the hell would you do watersports in the bedroom anyway?" I wrinkle my nose. That's something I really don't understand, and part of me feels like I'm missing something in the words.

A stifled laugh reverberates from behind the wooden desk, and I become acutely aware that Vinny is not alone in the room. *Oh, shit.*

My heart races, my cheeks blazing with heat, and I will the ground to swallow me whole.

I turn to face his three sons, two of them with smug grins on their faces, and the older one, Rafael, looks like he's about to have a coronary, with every vein in his corded neck protruding and his eyes alight with fury.

Oh, God.

"Someone needs to put their new toy in her place," Rafael says, glaring at me, and my eyebrows shoot up and my mouth falls open at his blatant rudeness.

"Don't worry, I will." Vinny's seething tone slices through me. He's pissed, really pissed.

My insides twist when I go over everything I said, so I close my eyes to block them out while I try and gain some sense of self-belief.

"I can help with the watersports question!" I snap my eyes open to lock eyes with his youngest son. Rocco sits with humor on his handsome face and his hand held up in the air like he's in a classroom.

"Don't you fucking dare!" Vinny erupts from his chair and throws himself over the desk toward Rocco, who just leans farther back in his chair, laughing wildly. "Get the fuck out of my office!" Vinny bellows, and I turn to make a quick exit.

"Gracie, you move another inch, and I swear to God,

you will not sit down for a month!" he warns. "The rest of you, out!"

The men all chuckle while I cling onto the wooden desk for support. *Oh, dear God, this is embarrassing.*

"Bye, Gracie, it was nice meeting you. Papa? Is she going to be my next stepmama?" Rocco asks, and my eyes almost shoot from their sockets. Vinny rushes toward him, his fists balled at his sides as Rafael pulls Rocco away and pushes him out the door. When the door slams behind them both, I swallow down my nervousness.

"Vinny?" I whisper, caressing his forearm, and his body eases against my touch. When our eyes connect, I feel like everything is right in the world.

There's something compassionate in his stare, something soft he keeps hidden, and as he bears his soul, I'm too enamored to realize I'm moving until he's shifted me into position between his legs and taken a seat.

Vinny

She's the perfect submissive, and she will become my disciplined pet, she just needs to sign those damn papers.

My eyes greedily work over her small body, and her fingers grip onto my arm, anchoring herself to the spot.

She still wears the same clothes from earlier—the blue sundress that makes her eyes appear so blue I could swim in them, and the cheap-looking flip-flops exposing her purple toenails, and I wonder if purple is her favorite color? Or is it blue?

Threading my fingers through her hair, I stroke the silky locks between my fingers, loving the way her breath hitches each time my bicep brushes her arm.

"Have you signed the forms?"

"N-no."

"No?" I crook an eyebrow.

"I have questions," she whispers.

With a heavy sigh, I lean back in my chair with one hand resting on her hip and the other stroking her smooth thigh beneath her sundress. "Go on," I drawl.

She clears her throat. "I didn't think you'd want to ..." Her eyes widen, and I chuckle at the way her face becomes red as she struggles to speak. *Jesus, I'm going to have so much fun with her.*

"You didn't think I'd want to fuck you again?" I smirk.

She swallows hard, then nods coyly.

"Why?"

"Well ..." She glances around the room like she expects someone else to jump out. "We're—I'm your—Robert is—"

I take pity on her and cut to the chase. "Robert is my stepson, and I'm widowed. I like to fuck, Gracie." She jolts at my words, but I continue. She needs to hear this. "While I admit I never normally go for much-younger women, there's something about you I like, and when I like something, I don't allow anything to stand in my way." I look at her pointedly. "Anything." She bites into her bottom lip, and fuck me, that move causes my bulge to thicken. I clear my throat. "So, I couldn't give less of a shit if you're Robert's long-lost daughter or not. I want you, therefore I will have you. I don't like the fact you've had another cock inside your pussy, but I'm going to erase all memory of that, do you understand?"

Her tongue sneaks out over her bottom lip, and my cock likes the action. So much so I lift my hips so the tip grazes my belt for some much-needed friction.

"Now. Sign. The. Fucking. Contract." I stab the papers with my finger, and she jumps, so I soften and place my hand back on her thigh, using my thumb to circle her exposed skin.

"But I have questions," she repeats the same as earlier.

"Questions?" I raise a brow.

"Uh-huh." She nods, and her hair covers her face like a drape.

Without warning, I lift her onto my desk and scoot my chair forward, allowing me to position myself between her open legs and cage her in.

"Ask," I demand, then wince at my deep growl.

She pushes her hair behind her ears. "Why?"

"Why what?"

"Why do you want a contract with me?"

I sigh heavily. "I already told you. I want to fuck you." She bites her bottom lip again, and I swear I almost erupt in my pants.

"Stop biting your bottom lip. Otherwise, I'll spank your ass even more than I planned on doing."

Her eyes widen and her blush deepens. "I-I'm not a child."

I chuckle loudly. "Damn right you're not." I trail my hand up her hip and over the swell of her tit, reveling in the way her nipple peaks beneath my touch. "I want the contract as security. In the past, I've had women attempt to blackmail me." She gasps, but I continue. "And I really don't want to put a bullet in your pretty little head for blackmailing me."

"I wouldn't." She shakes her head, and I want to crash my lips against her and plead with her to sign.

"Any more questions?"

"Watersports?" she asks.

I lean back in my chair and detach from her. "We can work up to that."

Her eyebrows furrow. "I don't understand."

I chuckle at her innocence. "It's piss play, Little Pet."

Her blue eyes widen. "Piss play?" Then her eyebrows shoot up, and her nose wrinkles. "Like peeing on me?"

"Or in you." I shrug.

"In me?" Her eyes widen further, and her mouth falls open.

"Hmm," I muse while dragging a finger over my lip, imagining swiping the tip of my dripping cock over her tight little nipple, then sucking the remnants from her.

"Like, actually inside me?"

My cock swells at the thought.

"Yes, then fucking you with my piss still warm inside your tight little hole." I nod.

"T-that's something you like." It's more of a statement than a question, and I grin before meeting her eyes.

"I like a lot of things, Little Pet. But yes, I'd like to fuck my little pet with warm piss inside her pussy."

Talking about it sends me into a frenzy. Fuck, I need her.

I push back on my chair and stand, forcing myself between her legs. Then I take a hold of the back of her head, tangling my hand in her hair, and slam my lips down on hers, giving her no choice but to give my tongue access to her mouth and allow me to devour her.

When I finally pull back, she's breathless and panting, my boxers are soaked in pre-cum, and I have a feral need to slam inside her pussy. "Sign the contract," I grunt out.

DOMINATION

Her tongue trails out over her lips, and she swallows. "Okay."

"Now!" I glance at the papers on the desk, and her eyes follow.

Then she leans to the side, remaining flush against me, and hope springs into my chest as she scribbles her signature on the paperwork, bringing me a deep sense of satisfaction.

And finally, I have my little pet.

Chapter Seven

Vinny

My hands work at the buttons on the side of her dress, popping them open, then she lifts her arms to allow me to slide it over her delectable body before dropping it to the floor.

She glances at the door. "Vinny, I ..."

"Daddy." I crook an eyebrow at her.

"Huh?"

I tilt my head toward the paperwork. "Daddy. You signed the paperwork. When we're going to have sex, you call me Daddy."

"Daddy ..." she whispers, trying it out on her tongue, and my cock jumps in delight.

"Red is your safe word, Little Pet. What is it?"

"Red."

"Good girl."

Her stunned lips part, and I can't help myself; I push my thumb into her mouth, and when she closes her soft lips around me, I'm left speechless, staring at her in awe. She's the most beautiful, innocent thing I've ever seen in my enter life.

Her bright-blue eyes spark with arousal, and I quickly unbuckle my pants to finally relieve myself.

"Daddy's thick cock is going to stretch you wide," I grunt.

"Oh, god," she pants, and I slide my thumb from her mouth.

My cock leaks as I pull it free, then I push her flimsy cotton panties to the side and delight in the way her wetness coats me. "My little pet is aroused, begging for Daddy's cock to please her."

She nods, and with my hand behind her head, I pull her toward me, nudging at her small entrance. "Beg Daddy, Little Pet. Beg Daddy to coat you with his cum."

Her heavy breaths fill the air, and I wait on tenterhooks for her agreement. "Say it," I bite.

"I-I want you to fill my pussy with your cum, Daddy."

"Good girl." I smile into her hair and push inside her tight little hole with a hiss. "Ffuuckk. My little pet is tight," I grind out.

She whimpers as I continue driving my thick length deep inside her, inch by punishing inch. "You're doing so good taking me," I breathe into her ear. "Such a big girl, taking all of Daddy's big cock."

"It hurts." She winces, and my chest puffs with pride. I know I'm big, yet she takes me so well it's like she was created just for me.

She clings to the nape of my neck as I thrust to the

hilt, and her small body jolts when I prod at the entrance of her cervix. There's something consuming about the fact I'm so deep inside her.

We're connected as one. As deep as I can possibly get inside the only person I've ever felt this connection with. I pull back to freefall into her eyes, and they shimmer with unshed tears, and her bottom lip wobbles. "It's okay, Little Pet. Daddy just wants to fill you," I coo, burying my face into her hair and breathing in her scent.

She nods and blinks away the tears as I palm the side of her face, then I slide back and forth inside her wet heat at a slow, sensual pace. Her pussy walls mold to me, and I bite the inside of my mouth as I consider I'm not the only man who has done this despite feeling like I am.

Jealousy spikes through me.

She's mine, and I'll kill anyone who tries to take her from me, anyone who dares to touch her. My pace picks up with each incoherent thought. Someone gave her a baby, the ultimate gift. The rattling of the desk is a sign of the power behind my movements as my thoughts unravel.

My hand wraps around her throat, and her pupils dilate. "You're mine, do you understand me?"

A moan of pleasure whooshes from her parted lips, and I thrust harder, emphasizing my statement.

"Oh. Oh, god, Daddy," she screams, and I duck my head, burying it into her neck, and sink my teeth into her skin, sucking hard and marking her as mine.

Something I've never done before.
Ever.

Gracie

The moment he wraps his thick hand around my throat, my orgasm hits me like a freight train. His body jolts in time with mine, then he buries his face in the crook of my neck and sinks his teeth into me. Stars dance in front of my eyes before his cum floods me and trickles between my asscheeks, but he continues thrusting, milking himself of every drop of cum, and coats me in his essence.

A chill racks through me at what I've just done. Holy shit, he came inside me.

"I-I'm not on birth control," I whisper, guilt forming in the pit of my stomach, and I tap his shoulder, hoping to grab his attention. He pushes his hips forward again. "I'm not on birth control. Daddy, stop! I'm not on birth control."

I swear I feel him smile into my neck, but when he pulls back to focus on me, his face is a mask of indifference.

A tear falls from my eye as his gaze roams over my face. "Shhh, Little Pet. Daddy will sort this. I have a doctor on hand. He can sort this for us, don't cry, okay?" His smooth voice should relax me, but the thought of him having doctors on hand sends a rush of jealousy and anger through me. How often does this happen for him? Am I not his only pet?

I push him back, but he doesn't budge, only angering me further.

Then he grips my hair and yanks my head back, causing my neck to stretch while I blink back the shock of his rough action. "Little Pet. Behave. I said I'd sort it, and I will. Now, Daddy's going to pull out of you, then you're going to lick my desk clean as I spank you for misbehaving."

My eyes bounce over his face. "What the?"

He wrenches my hair again, and I cry out. "Behave. I'm going to look after you," he warns, so I attempt to nod. "Good girl," he croons, and I'm so conflicted. His words are such a contrast to his actions, but I want to please him.

When he slides his cock from me, I miss the feeling of being stretched, filled, and needed. Not giving me a chance to dwell on it, he spins me to face the desk, pulls my ass back, and tears my panties off me. Forcing my neck against the mahogany desk, he says, "Lick."

A sharp crack fills the air, then, as if distracted by the sounds, his slap burns my skin. "Lick!"

Oh, shit.

There's not a lot but enough to leave a mess. I swipe my tongue through the cum. It's salty and warm and tastes of him.

"Good Little Pet, cleaning up your mess. Keep licking."

Smack!

A sob bubbles in my throat, but strangely, my clit throbs as he strokes over my heated ass. The forbidden nature behind our actions has me eager to comply.

Smack!

Again, I lick at the wood. My pussy drips with desire at how utterly filthy this is, but for once in my life, I feel like I'm being controlled in the best way. This is as much about my pleasure as it is about his.

Smack!

"Hmm, I can't wait to fuck this ass, Little Pet." His hands tighten on the globes of my ass, pulling them apart, then I hear him spit before it lands in the crook of my ass. "Fuck, your ass will look divine leaking with my cum."

My clit throbs, begging to be toyed with. "Please."

"Do you like being Daddy's slut, Little Pet?"

Oh, god, I do.

"Y-yes."

His thick fingers move between my legs, and I stifle a sob of relief. "Keep licking away my cum, Little Pet, while Daddy plays with you and your sopping pussy."

Holy shit, that feels good. His rough fingers circle my clit, pressing it with each stroke, and my tongue becomes as wild as his touch. "That's it, lick my cum. Clean up my mess."

Lightning lust zips up my spine, causing me to clench my pussy, and I freefall into the throes of desire, begging and pleading with more of his mess to clean.

To please my daddy like a good little pet.

Chapter Eight

Vinny

Her legs give way the moment I withdraw my fingers from her tight hole, and my cock is once again rock hard just from hearing her orgasm.

I pick up my girl bridal style and pull her against my chest, her eyes are hazy, and she falls lax in my hold. A slow smile spreads over her pretty face, so I take my time to analyze her features. Her lips pout into a bow shape and the freckles over her face twitch as she stares back at me with something akin to love in her eyes, but that can't be right, can it?

The thought breaks my moment, and I stride through my office, then foyer and take two steps at a time until I reach her bedroom. I deposit her on the bed, then head toward her bathroom. "W-what are you doing?" Her voice filters through the sound of the running taps, and I dump a squirt of bubbles into the tub.

"Aftercare."

"Huh? What?"

I poke my head around the door. "Aftercare. If you'd read the fucking contract fully, you'd understand." My tone is full of accusation, but it shouldn't be surprising. It's become evident Gracie hasn't done her research.

She rolls her eyes, and annoyance rushes through me, so I turn back to the tub. My irritation is short-lived when she appears in the doorway in nothing more than her cotton bra, bare pussy on display for me. The slickness between her legs, her hair giving just-fucked vibes, and a gleam of wetness coating her chin have my balls aching with a need to be satisfied. Again.

"I can take care of myself." She leans against the door jamb.

"It's my job to take care of you, Little Pet."

She tilts her head, and I swirl the bubbles around with my hand. "Why do you like to have pets?" She chews on her lip.

I've been asked this question countless times over the years, but I've never given an honest response, shying away from opening up, yet with her, I find myself wanting to be truthful. I want to be me, and more so, I want her to like me.

I clear my throat. "You know I'm a Mafia don, right? Your father told you?"

She nods.

"My world is dangerous and cruel, and I had to make a sacrifice very early on in life in order for me to become the man I am today, and that sacrifice was affection, love. It's not something we can afford to have."

She swallows hard but maintains eye contact. "But

what about your sons? You love them, right?" Her voice is soft, almost a whisper but not quite.

"I do. They're my everything. But I've taught them what I was taught. They just chose not to use it." My lip twitches at the thought of my sons ignoring my advice and forging their own paths, and honestly, I couldn't be happier for them. I'm proud they insisted on taking women they love as their wives; something I never did. At the time, I thought that was the right option for me. Now? Not so much.

She wrings her hands in front of her. "My father said you've been married before. Did you not love your wives?"

"No, I didn't." I don't shy away from telling her the truth. She needs to hear it and needs to know whatever she's feeling will not be reciprocated on my part. "The closest I came was to your grandmother, Nancy. But that was more of a companionship."

For the first time during our conversation, she flicks her eyes away before bringing them back to me. "My father says you had an arrangement with his mother. Did you have sex with her?"

"Yes."

Her breath hitches, and I hate I might have hurt her, but I'm not a liar and have nothing to hide.

"Was she your pet?"

I drag a hand through my hair, uncomfortable with this line of questioning. If I answer truthfully, she will think there's more to it than what there was when there isn't.

"No. She wasn't."

Her shoulders sag and her face falls, and I'm on my feet in an instant to reassure her. I tuck her soft locks behind her ears, then tilt her chin up to face me.

"Nancy was good with my boys. She was a single mother and started out as a housekeeper, but I knew she was falling for me, and I told myself not to go there. When one of my wives tried to kidnap Rafael, she put herself in front of her and took the sharp end of a knife." She sucks in a sharp breath, but I continue on.

"She saved my son from a deadly blackmail plot that would have left him dead. When I asked her if she wanted to quit working but said I would still provide for her as a thank you, she said she enjoyed taking care of us, but asked if I would have sex with her so she knew what it felt like to have a part of me, if only for an hour." I don't tell her I had to imagine it was someone else I was fucking at the time because there was no spark.

"We didn't have sex again. It's like she knew my head wasn't in it, and my heart sure as fuck wasn't. When she was diagnosed with terminal cancer, I told her again to quit working, but she refused. I asked her what she wanted, and she said my hand in marriage. For Robert to have our protection, the protection of a good man that gave his heart to others." I laugh, but it lacks humor. "I don't give my heart to anyone, Little Pet. Your grandmother was deluded, much like your father."

A tear slips down her face, and I swipe it away. "At least this way, when I have little pets, they know their place. I'm not lying to them; I'm not professing my love nor having sex while they bat their lashes at me with hearts in their eyes. I get to take care of them like they crave, and I can give affection without the risk of enemies seeking retribution. I can protect them without declaring my love for them, and I can treat them exactly as the contract states, as nothing more than a pet."

Her chest rises. "You deserve more than that too, Vinny, and I think my grandmother was right, you have a heart," she whispers. Her words are like a dagger through my chest, twisting with a cruel hand, so I pull away from her, spinning back toward the bathtub.

"It's Daddy," I snap, then regret it. Exhaling, I soften my tone. "Now, come, get in." I hold my hand out for her, and when our eyes reconnect, the sadness that was there moments ago is replaced with a steely determination.

One I'm not sure I'm prepared for.

Chapter Nine

Gracie

Unfortunately, I never got to meet my paternal grandmother, and while I regret that because she sounds like a wonderful person, I'm also grateful. Mainly because I would've had to deal with my father for even longer than I have already.

To say I was relieved Vinny didn't have sexual feelings toward her is an understatement. It's not lost on me how fucked-up my situation is, and as much as I'd like to say I'm not doing this with him, I simply can't. We're connected somehow, like we both know this is happening, so we just go with it. He's like the missing piece of my puzzle, and although he's old enough to be my grandparent, I don't care. Not a single part of me cares.

He says he doesn't love, but he proves it in the way he cares for me, even if I am just a pet. He's shown he's capable of compassion and tenderness, and he's admitted he loves his sons. Yet he refuses to be vulnerable with a woman, or allow a woman to be vulnerable with him maybe?

Well, I'd like to test my theory. Vincent Marino may be the head of a notorious Mafia family—dangerous, controlling, and fearsome—but he's also my daddy—controlling, caring and giving.

My hand slides into his thick one, then he leans forward on his knees, grasps my hips, and brings my body flush to his face. His breath fans my pussy as he places a kiss on my bare mound. The tickle of his cropped beard makes me giggle, so I pull back, holding his gaze, and unclip my bra, drop it to my feet, then turn and sashay over to the tub. I make a languorous show of stepping into the bubbles, ensuring he can see my slick folds wet with his cum.

Vinny

After washing her hair, I work my way down her body with a sponge. I barely got a chance to view her tits before she sank beneath the bubbles, but when I slide the suds over her shoulder and down her neck, I take extra care in handling her tit. It's the perfect size in my hand, and it's grown so much, thanks to the birth of her daughter.

The thought of the adorable baby girl sleeping in her nursery has anger coursing through me, causing me to grind my teeth.

"What's wrong?"

"Do you love him?"

Her eyes bounce over my face.

"Do you love him?" I ask again, sterner this time.

"Who?"

"Bonnie's father." I wait with bated breath, holding the swell of her tit in my palm.

"No." She shakes her head. "I don't love him." She's lying. I can see it in the way her pupils shine, the quick movement of her gaze, and how she pulls her lip into her mouth immediately after.

Jealousy thrashes through me in unrelenting surges, infecting my bloodstream as I consider who this punk is. He's no doubt much younger than me and not in the Mafia. Hell, he can offer her everything a young woman is meant to have.

Then I remember Robert him telling me he used drugs and was abusive, and it gives me the perfect excuse to ban her from seeing him again, Bonnie too.

"I don't want him around you or Bonnie." With my free hand, I turn her to face me. "Do you understand? He's not to touch you. Either of you." I don't understand the possessiveness ravishing my bloodstream, but I know without a shadow of doubt that they're both mine, and no fucker will take them from me.

She nods but doesn't seem convinced. "If he lays a single finger on you, Gracie, I'll slaughter him." A whimper leaves her throat, but I ignore it. "Nobody touches you but me. Do you understand me?" I pinch her chin harder.

Air slips from her lips. "I understand."

Her words send a flurry of relief through me, so I release her chin. "Good girl, Little Pet." I nuzzle into her hair, showering her in praise. "Such a good girl for Daddy."

"What about you?"

I still my movements and pull back to face her.

"What about me?"

"Are you going to let anyone else touch you?"

I chuckle, scanning her face. Her wet hair clings to

her, and I can't wait to brush it for her while she sits on my lap. "Nobody but you," I state, and a gracious smile spreads across her face, a beautiful fucking smile that has my chest filling with a foreign feeling of happiness usually reserved solely for my family.

That's what she is, I tell myself. She's family already, that's why I feel the connection with her when I've never before.

The thought of someone else touching me fills me with irritation. Quite frankly, since fucking Gracie, I've been unable to bear anyone else's touch.

A loud wail has her startling and shocking the hell out of me when she springs up from the bath in a wild panic.

"She needs to be fed. Oh, god, she's not had her evening milk." She practically jumps over the tub and grabs a towel, and I remain on the bathroom floor transfixed how she became so frantic at the cry of her daughter. Hell, one of my wives refused to deal with crying children full-stop, and another insisted on having a nanny until the children learned not to cry. I put a bullet in her head for ever implying such a stupid thing.

"Do you want me to do something?" I ask, desperate to help settle them both.

Like what? I don't fucking know, but again, I want to be there for her. To be more.

"No, thank you." My shoulders slump. "I breastfeed!" she shouts back, and it takes a moment for my mind to compute her words.

Breastfeed?

As in? The milk comes from her tits.

Holy shit.

I choke on thin air.

This I must see, and it appears so does my fucking cock because it's now back to full height at the thought of the milk leaking from her tit. My balls throb and the head of my cock releases a steady flow of glistening pre-cum.

Standing, I adjust myself, knowing damn well it's not okay to be hard in the vicinity of a child. Then I throw open the bedroom door, and the moment my eyes latch onto the scene before me, I almost swallow my tongue.

Holy. Fuck.

I need a new contract.

One that keeps her tied to me forever.

Chapter Ten

Gracie

Vinny's free hand follows each stroke of the hairbrush gliding through my silky blonde hair all the way to my ass.

When he stepped in the doorway from the bathroom to find me feeding Bonnie on the bed, he looked like he was about to pass out, and I couldn't help but giggle. His expression was priceless, and when I teased that he was acting like he'd seen no one breastfeed before, he told me he's never been in the same room as someone feeding. I slow-blinked at his reply; surely, I didn't him right.

He told me his children's mothers refused to breast-fed, and I immediately felt bad for them. Had they been starved of affection too? Yet Vinny practically showers me with love. Even if he can't see it yet, I see it in his eyes, in the way he masks his emotions to make me feel secure, and in the way he changes his tone of voice when I jump at his aggressiveness.

He watched from the corner of the room while I fed Bonnie, and his deep, hungry stare made me feel like I was being devoured without even being touched. Every cell in my body was alight under the blazing heat of his gaze.

"Has she finished?" His raspy voice sends a ripple of desire through me, and all I can do is nod. "Take her to the nursery, then come back here." He points between his legs, and I slide off the bed with Bonnie in my arms. Her cute little pout has me leaning down to kiss her soft waves, and as I slip her into her crib, her lips part on a soft whimper that has happiness creeping up my throat.

"Night, baby girl," I whisper, and lean into her crib to deliver her another kiss while covering her with her fleece blanket. She doesn't so much as murmur when I tiptoe out of her room, and I leave the door slightly ajar. I'm not used to being away from her at night, so it helps with my anxiety of her being in her own room.

Then I do just as Vinny asked and make my way between his parted legs. The man is sex on a stick, and his hungry gaze has heat surging through me, leaving me a wanton mess between my thighs.

It was only a short while ago that he filled me, but I want a repeat. Would I ever get enough of him? And him of me? The thought has my heart seizing.

"Have you read the contract yet?" He crooks a mocking brow in my direction.

"Most of it," I mutter.

"Then you know I expect you to bow at my feet."

Bow at his feet? What does he think this is, the 1800s?

DOMINATION

"What if I don't?" I pout, knowing damn well what happens if I break the rules. In fact, I'm counting on it. According to his contract, I will be spanked, so I'm waiting for it to happen.

As if knowing my reasoning, his lip curls. I want to stroke his handsome face, but instead, I remain silent, waiting for him to bend me over his knee, pull down my sleep shorts, and spank my ass. The thought of his rough hand on my delicate skin makes me come alive with fervor.

"I'll take you to my dungeon and leave you begging for pleasure." He glares back at me, and my eyes widen.

"D-dungeon?" I don't remember reading anything about a dungeon.

He nods slowly and his lip twitches. Nervousness hits me, and for the first time, I worry about what I've gotten myself into. Can I do this? A dungeon? I've gone from being naïve and trusting, to being thrust into a world I barely know anything about, a world I was eager to remove myself from.

Still, I tell myself I will be leaving soon, so I might as well have a little fun before I start my new life as far away from so-called family as possible.

"I'll leave your little pussy dripping in my cum, begging for me to fill you like a desperate little whore." My breath hitches, sticking in my throat, but he continues. "I can't decide if I want my little pet caged or chained to a bench." He chuckles, and my mouth drops open. *He can't be serious?* "Now, make your choice." He muses, dragging his forefinger over his lip. Something tells me either of them would satisfy him.

Slowly, I lower to the floor, reveling in the way his fingers grip the chair's arm, and he sucks in a deep breath. Then I lower my head, like I saw in a movie.

"Good, Little Pet. Such a good girl for Daddy." He strokes my head, and I could weep at the way the gesture warms my insides. "Climb on Daddy's lap and let me see you," he rumbles, as if it's painful for him to speak so gently. The hairbrush has been discarded, long forgotten.

When I get to my feet, he reaches out. "Let Daddy take these off." His voice is low and full of care, and he slides his fingers into the sides of my sleep shorts and lowers them to the floor. "Good." He sits back in his chair and pats his thigh.

Leaning over him, I hold onto his shoulders and climb onto his lap so I'm straddling his waist. His chest is rising rapidly, and I blush at his reaction to me. My fingers dig into the shoulders of his white dress shirt, and my legs rest on his thighs. He wraps one arm behind my back, then lowers it to grip my ass cheek. I bite into my bottom lip, trying not to moan against his touch. The heat of his thick, calloused palm burns through me. Then he slaps my ass hard, causing me to jolt. "Take your top off, I want to try your milk."

His words stun me, leaving me breathless, and I sink into the depths of his murky-gray eyes for reassurance. A growl erupts from his throat. "Little *Pet*"—he drags the latter out—"you're making me angry. Just do as I say like a good girl." A sharp slap echoes in the air, then he caresses the flaming skin of my ass, causing me to wince.

Without needing further prompting, I lift my lacy camisole over my head and drop it to the floor. He hisses between his teeth at my tits bouncing freely, and I roll my lip into my mouth to stop myself from smiling.

Why do I want to please this man so much? Why when I laid eyes on the man who is my father's stepfather, did I not quiver in fear and run from the dangerous glint in his eyes? Why do I crave his touch, beg for his approval? Why do I want him to love me?

"Shhh, Little Pet." He presses his finger to my lips, and his eyes darken as he studies me with such scrutiny my heart clenches, stealing the oxygen from my lungs. It's like he's searching my soul, revealing the lies and secrets hidden there, and disabling my plans before I can even put them into action.

"I own you, Little Pet. You're mine." The words roll off his tongue like a possessive threat, a vow, and I swallow back the fear wedged in my chest and give in to the way his rough hand lifts my breast to his mouth. He kisses my breast before wrapping his lips around my nipple and sucking, his eyes never leaving mine.

"Feed Daddy, Little Pet," he growls, and wetness slides from my pussy, and I swear I feel him smile against me.

Vinny

Warm milk splashes onto my tongue, and my eyes roll at the splendor of her taste before coming back to her innocent face. This close to her, I can make out the small freckles scattered lightly over her nose. My hand squeezes her plump tit, reveling in the way she arches her back as she feeds me.

Fuck. The thought of her providing milk for me has me feeling feral.

For me. Not the douche who knocked her up.

This is not something I've done before, but the moment I knew she could, I wanted it, I wanted a part of her she only gives to the person she loves most in the world. I wanted to taste what no man had tasted before me. A thought flashes through my mind, and fury beats at my chest, so I detach from her nipple with a pop. Removing my hand from her ass, I grab a hold of her hair, tug her head back, and sneer down at her. "Have you let your fuckboy taste these tits?" I snarl.

Her mouth falls open, and she attempts to shake her

head, but my fingers tighten in her hair enough to pinch her scalp. "N-no, Daddy." The fact she remembers to address me accordingly settles something inside me, and knowing she hasn't fed him from her tit has me wanting to beat my chest like a goddamn drum with my fists.

"Good girl." I release her hair, and like a frenzied animal, I take both her tits in my hands, loving the way they spill over my thick palms, and push them together. "You only let Daddy feed from them."

"Y-yes."

My cock weeps with satisfaction. "Take Daddy's cock out, Little Pet. I want you to shove it in your tight little cunt while you feed me. Only you can give Daddy what he needs."

"Oh, god," she pants, her tits being pushed farther into my mouth. My tongue lashes over her peaked nipples, sucking them both at once. Her milk flows like a jet stream, and I struggle to swallow it all back, so it leaks from the corners of my mouth, and I growl at the thought of losing it.

Her small hands unbuckle my pants, and when she pulls my solid cock from my boxers, I squeeze my eyes closed to ward off the orgasm her gentle touch coaxes. "Fuck," I grunt, and buck my hips. "Slide your cunt down." I nip at the flesh around her nipple in warning. "Slide your wet pussy down on my cock, Little Pet." I draw her nipple into my mouth and guzzle.

The tip of my cock nudges at her entrance, and her chest heaves as she lowers herself on my length. Fuck, that's good. My eyes roll when I feed harder, my tongue lashing over her nipple after each generous ounce of milk slides down my throat. "Good girl," I croon, stroking her hair.

A thousand sensations of pleasure zip through me, each combining with the other and bringing with it a desperate need to be satiated. My hips thrust up hard, and I use the grip on her ass to slam her down on my length. A scream rushes from her, and her pussy clenches unbelievably tight around me as a splurge of liquid coats my cock. "Oh, fuck." I bounce her on my cock again and again, rougher, and her tits slap me in the face. My little pet squirting coats my balls in her wetness, and I smack her ass hard. "Dirty little slut."

"Yes, Daddy." She moans, and the sound vibrates through me. Her compliance is enough to push me over the edge, and as my cum is milked from my cock, my eyes roll to the back of my head, and with a mouth full of her milk, I give myself over to the feeling of bliss.

I'm lost in my girl, my beautiful little pet, and I'm keeping her.

Chapter Eleven

Gracie

Opening my eyes, I groan at attempting to sit up, finding I'm unable to due to the thick arm banded around my chest and clutching at my breast as if it's a prized possession. With an achy body, a smile tugs on my lips, and I trail my finger over the silver hairs on his muscular olive-toned arms. His solid form rests against my back in a protective manner, and I embrace the feeling, a comfort it seems only he can provide.

His cock inside me is somehow hard. I'm not sure when that happened, but being stretched around him makes me feel completely and utterly full of someone's devotion. Tracing his weathered tattoos covering his bicep, I inhale his pinewood cologne, wishing the scent would imprint in my lungs and live there.

Sure, he may be older than me, but his body is impressive. After fucking me in the chair last night, he carried me to the bed, used my camisole to tie my wrists to the headboard, then opened my legs wide and pushed them up to my face, leaving me exposed and dripping with his cum while he fucked his hand. With his jaw clenched, he guided himself inside me at a steady pace. Inch by cruel inch, he slid inside me, staring down at my stretched hole. My nipples were peaked and leaking, and the wild gleam in his eyes bordered on sinister as he snapped his hips back, then thrust deeper inside me; so deep he hit my cervix. Pain mixed with pleasure, and the determined look on his face told me he knew it too.

When my body finally gave out, he continued to rock back and forth during my unconsciousness, and I didn't have it in me to care. Besides, the damn contract probably states he can do as he pleases when he pleases. I had, after all, signed my soul over to the devil himself without so much as a care in the world. Why should I? This was all temporary. "A means to an end" as my father called it.

"Will Bonnie need fed this morning?" His gruff voice causes my chest to tighten. I hadn't realized he was awake while I admired his impressive body.

"No. She just likes to feed at night, like a comfort thing. It's why I become so full." My cheeks heat, and I'm grateful he can't see my reaction.

Him commanding my body, every part of it, has stirred a submissiveness inside me I never knew existed. Part of me wants to hate my body's dependency I seem to have on him. It can't be a good thing, especially given my plans, but the other part of me thrives on it, willing it to happen.

His thumb grazes my nipple, and I glance down to watch it. Milk bubbles from me, a distinctively erotic sight that causes me to push back on his impressive cock now deepening inside me.

He buries his head in the crook of my neck and places gentle kisses below my ear. "I love seeing my collar on you."

My mind whirls his words around until I realize what he said, then my hand moves to my neck. Sure enough, leather encompasses my neck. I stiffen at the foreign feeling, then relax at the happiness flooding me at belonging, being wanted and of need to someone.

When the hell did this happen?

A loud chuckle leaves his chest. "Hmm, you're so hot when you're confused, Little Pet." I hadn't realized I'd voiced my thoughts. "It happened last night after you begged me to make you mine forever. I took off my belt and used my knife to make it the perfect size."

I said that? He used his belt to collar me? I shake my head, my mind spinning at the night's events. "Don't worry, Little Pet. I'm keeping you." He nips at my throat, then drives his cock into me so hard I've no choice but to cling to his arm for support. His sinister laugh fills the air, and he moves so quick I'm left stunned. My back hits the mattress, and he plows into me, causing the headboard to slam against the wall. "That's it. Fuck, that's it. Squeeze Daddy's cock. Fuck, I love filling your tight little cunt with my baby."

His words wash over me like a bucket of ice water, and my blood goes cold. He knows I'm not on birth control. His hips move quicker, my body simply a tool for his task.

He can't be serious? This is not part of my plan.

The punishing way his hips pound against me snoozes the warning siren going off in my mind, and I give myself over to him and the incredible sensations he elicits in me.

When he grinds his hips, my body becomes his, and my pussy clenches, holding onto him tightly. "Filling your cunt with my baby, Little Pet." His eyes darken, his jaw clenches, then the roar from his chest is followed by his body stilling and his cock pulsating thick ropes of hot-white cum into me. "That's it, breed for me," he rasps.

Vinny

My arms give way, and I hit the mattress. Thankfully, I have the foresight to roll, taking her with me when I do. Her heart hammers against mine, and I stroke over her golden locks. It's as soothing for me as it is her.

"I have a business meeting in two hours, but I don't want to move." I chuckle at the irrational thought. Under normal circumstances, I fuck my little pets and leave their beds to go back to my own.

"Hmm, I don't want you to," she pouts.

I lift my head to look down at her, her bright-blue eyes are glazed over, and she looks sleepy, satiated. "Such a beautiful little pet." Maybe I should bend the rules for her, just for today. As quick as the thought enters my head, I banish it. That shit will get me in trouble, and ultimately, her too. So I tap her ass. "Up. I'm showering while you sort Bonnie, then leave her with Hazel while you do your morning routine."

Her head pops up and her eyebrows draw together. The confusion on her face is adorable.

"With Hazel? What morning routine?" Her voice becomes higher on each word.

"Tsk, tsk, Little Pet." I slide from beneath her, pulling the sheet from her body. Then I slap her ass, knowing damn well it will leave a mark on her. "Read the fucking contract!" I soften at the way her face crumbles. "Hazel is trained in looking after babies. She has first aid certification among a dozen other things." I throw my arm out.

She rolls onto her back to face me, and my footing wavers. Unable to help myself, I tap her thigh. "Open." She complies immediately, and my cock hardens at the sight of my thick white cum spilling from her small pussy hole, her folds coated in my essence. Fuck, that's good. I pump my cock with one hand, imagining embedding my seed deep inside her and ensuring she's my little pet for a lifetime.

I scoop my cum up with two fingers, then shove them deep inside her, and a stuttered gasp leaves her lips. "I don't want any going to waste." I wink.

I grin, meeting her gaze, and slide my fingers from inside her. Stepping toward her, I take a hold of her chin. "Open." Her small lips part, and arousal floods me at pushing my fingers into her mouth. "Suck." Her mouth hollows, and her tongue works over my digits, causing my cock to leak ropes of pre-cum against my stomach muscles. "Fuck, that's good." Reluctantly, I draw them out, and her doe eyes peer up at me with something akin to disappointment lacing them.

"Vinny, you said yesterday you'd organize the morning-after pill."

And like that, she's obliterated my arousal. My

nostrils flare, and I spin to face her, the anger flowing through my veins is like a toxic spill overtaking everything alive and destroying it in its wake. Every muscle in my body clenches. She's already planning on this not being permanent and leaving, probably to run off with Bonnie's father. Over my dead fucking body. I always get what I want, and what I want is her.

"I'll organize a doctor today." My tone is clipped, and her eyes flash with worry, but I don't have it in me to care despite knowing I should. I give my head a shake, then swing open the bedroom door and head to my room. She's not the only one who's broken my routine, I did so willingly. I don't want to shower her scent off me, her pussy juice still coats my cock, and I want nothing more than to leave it there, where it belongs.

Hazel walks past me with cleaning products in her hand and doesn't even bat an eye at my naked form. She's used to it with how long she's been working here. "I want her ready and at my feet in thirty minutes," I snipe out.

"Yes, sir. Would you like her naked?"

I glance over my shoulder and lock eyes with her. Why the fuck would she ask me such a stupid question? "Of course." I glare for added effect, and the poor woman jolts.

She gives me a curt nod, but I don't miss the flash of disapproval in her eyes. Does she seriously think Gracie is different from the other women I've housed over the years?

Well, she's not, I tell myself, but the moment I do, I regret it. The room feels bare, lifeless, her scent doesn't hang in the air like I want it to. Her softness isn't in here.

My chest constricts, and I rub over my heart. Why the fuck is this happening to me now? "Fuck!" My lungs vibrate against my chest, and my temple pounds. I swipe the contents of my dresser onto the floor and storm toward my shower. I'm about to wash her scent off me, then remind her and myself she's nothing more than my little pet to toy with.

When I enter the breakfast room a little over thirty minutes later, I'm still rolling up the sleeves to my white shirt. My forearms are thick with muscle, but now that I'm older, my skin is slightly weathered, and the hairs on my arms are as silver as the ones on my head. A sign of my age that I don't need reminded of. Not when I have Rocco, my youngest son, to remind me every fucking time he's in my presence. It's another reason the girl kneeling on the floor in the breakfast room should not be with a man like me, not permanently at least. Though my mind is at battle with itself, telling me this is unethical and she and her daughter deserve better, I've already decided I intend on keeping her.

They deserve a future, one that isn't short-lived.

Ignoring her presence, I continue my precise morning routine and head to the refrigerator for my morning smoothie. I flip the cap and guzzle it down, then power on the coffee machine. Leaning, I grab two freshly baked croissants from the counter and place them on my plate along with the small dish of butter and jelly. After setting them on a tray along with my coffee and the fresh glass of orange juice I instructed to be waiting for her this morning, I head into the breakfast room overlooking the patio.

Usually, I would leave the door open, uncaring who sees me enjoying my morning, but unwilling to let anyone see her but me, I close the door. I take a seat at the glass table while trying to ignore the adrenaline thrashing through my veins like liquid fire, thanks to her compliance.

It's a higher table than normal, one designed by my specifications, so I can see her small naked body bent over, with her head resting on her lap as instructed. Good, at least she's been reading.

Taking a sip of the coffee, I cut into my croissant, and my jaw flexes in annoyance. "You're supposed to unzip my pants and suck on my cock right about now," I clip out.

Her head pops up, and her gaze lands on me, causing my breath to constrict with the innocence shining in her eyes. Jesus, I'm a bastard.

When her hand glides my zipper down, I couldn't give less of a shit what I am; all that matters is her soft hand on my thick cock.

There's a tremble to her touch, and when I push a bite of the croissant past my lips, I almost choke on the buttery flakes as she surveys my cock in her hand and licks her lips like someone in awe, like a hungry little whore. "Mouth," I prompt with a lift of my chin, and she nods, directing my cock toward her sweet lips.

If she wasn't so small, she wouldn't be able to nod from beneath the table. It's almost like I had her in mind when bringing this table to life.

Her warm mouth encompasses me, and a thrill zips up my spine. "Good. Good girl," I croon, and her wide eyes beam up at me as I push my hips forward, careful not to choke her. Not yet at least.

"Keep sucking while I eat. Daddy wants to feed you." She nods, and I smirk at the muffled sound vibrating my cock when her little tongue swirls over the angry head. "That's it. Get it nice and wet." *Fuck, that's good.* I lift my hips with a grunt, and her tongue dips into my slit. This will be difficult. How the hell am I supposed to eat while she's sucking on me so damn well, and why the fuck does this feel better than any blowjob I've had before. Her swollen, stretched lips are a sight for sore eyes. They're my undoing.

"Keep sucking," I encourage, tightening my grip around my coffee cup. "Keep sucking. Lick me clean when you've finished." I push my hips forward, and she's bobbing her head, slurping around my length. She's found a rhythm she's enjoying. "That's it. Suck me harder." Her ass moves back and forth as she rocks her body, and I imagine how good a dildo would look stretching her ass wide open while I take her little cunt in one of my clubs. "Don't stop sucking, filthy Little Pet," I growl. Unable to hold back any longer and with little warning, my hot cum splashes into her mouth, and she chokes. I slam my cup down, and the hot coffee spills over my hand when I shift my hips to meet her mouth.

My chest heaves, and my hands ball into fists at the most spectacular orgasm crashing into me, then I lock eyes with hers. With tears streaming down her cheeks and her mouth stuffed with my thick cock, the beast inside me roars to be released. I've never felt like this before, ever.

I don't become possessive over anything, never have, but from the moment I laid eyes on her at the party over a year ago, she unlocked something inside of me I never knew existed.

She swirls her tongue over the head of my cock, then down my shaft to my balls, cleaning me up just as I commanded, and I will myself not to become hard again, not with such a long day ahead of me; I don't have time for this.

Without warning her, I slip my cock inside my boxers, then zip up my pants and shift my legs to the side. "Come." I hold out my hand for her, and when her unsure eyes meet me and her soft palm slides into mine, I have a wild need to reassure her. "You did very good, Little Pet. Let Daddy feed you more for being a good girl."

She nods, and a smile spreads over her lips as she rises from beneath the table.

"Do I need to do that every morning?" she asks, and I lift her onto my lap, wrap an arm around her slender waist, then push a small portion of the croissant into her mouth.

"You didn't read the contract." It's an accusation, not a question, but she replies anyway.

"I'm getting through it," she snipes out, with fire behind her eyes that was absent only moments ago.

My lip twitches at her feistiness, not something I'm used to. My hand on her hip tightens. "Don't snap back.

I'll spank your ass, and I have a busy day ahead of me, so I don't have time for it."

Her chastised gaze meets mine, oozing in self-pity. "I'm sorry."

"Good girl. Now eat." I lift more croissant to her mouth, and my cock hardens at her lips brushing over the tips of my fingers.

"And in answer to your question. When I fuck you at night, I expect you at my feet in the morning as a thank you." I feed her another portion and follow it up with holding the glass of orange juice to her lips, delighting in the swallow of the juice down her slender throat.

"Normally, when I've finished feeding this greedy mouth"—I swipe the juice from her lips and tear another portion of the croissant off to feed her—"I send my little pet back to wherever she came from. But seeing as though you're staying here ..." I want to tell her permanently, but I don't want to terrify her when she's being so compliant. "Once we've finished with breakfast, you can go and get showered and dressed, then collect Bonnie from Hazel."

"Can I take her to a park?"

My gaze narrows on her and her hopeful face. There's no fucking way I'm risking her going to a park without me. Someone like her will be every fucker's wet dream. Nope, she's vulnerable and sheltered, something I have Robert to thank for, possibly the only thing I want to thank him for—delivering me the sweetest girl to walk the earth.

"We have gardens here. There's no reason for you to leave the grounds." Her shoulders slump, so I quickly feel the need to make it up to her. "No park today, at least. Maybe another time." Lies, all fucking lies; there's no way she's leaving me.

I slide her off my lap and onto the chair, allowing me to stand. Then my gaze zeros in on her heavy tits, making it difficult for me to leave the room. My phone rings from my pants pocket, and I sigh, knowing Massio is waiting. I shoot him a quick text to tell him I'll be five minutes, then I silence it and turn my focus back to the little beauty at the breakfast table. My very naked little beauty, for all to see.

I glance toward the kitchen, hating the fact my men could potentially see her like this. "Fuck!" I grab my suit jacket from off the back of the chair. "Here, I don't want you walking round the house naked. From now on, you're to wear a robe around the house until I instruct you otherwise."

"But ..." I glare at her, then she clamps her mouth shut and gifts me with a nod. The thought of leaving her here has me feeling like I'm abandoning her, and a strange sense of unease washes over me. Lifting her arms one at a time like you would a child, I guide them into my jacket and internally smile when I see the way it buries her, covering up everything I don't want others to see. I make a mental note to have security only entering the house when cleared by myself.

"If I call you, you answer, do you understand me?" I look at her pointedly.

"I-I don't have a cell phone."

I rear back. What nineteen-year-old doesn't have a cellphone? "You don't have a cell phone?" She shakes her head, and I rub my bottom lip. Maybe Robert was protecting her, cutting her off from the guy who knocked her up and abandoned her. Another thing to thank the sly fucker for, it seems. "I'll have one delivered to you within the hour."

"But you don't have—" I press my finger to her lips, and her eyes widen.

"When I gift you with something, I expect a 'Thank you, Daddy.'"

Lust fills her eyes, and she practically sways on the chair, and as soon as I remove my finger, she opens her mouth. "Thank you, Daddy."

I suck in a sharp intake of air. "Good girl." I stroke her silky hair. "Now, I'll be back later." Then I lean down, inhale her peach scent, and place a kiss on the top of her head.

As I head through the door toward Massio, the sound of Bonnie giggling has me stilling. Every part of me wants to turn around and spend the day with her and her mother, but as always, the Mafia waits for no one, least of all their Don.

Chapter Twelve

Vinny

"Where the hell have you been?" Rafael spits out the moment I enter the room. Anger rolls off him like a tsunami. His face is red, and the vein on his neck is protruding. I slowly slip into my seat at the head of the table, ignoring his outburst, and take my time checking my phone and emails. I'm riling him up further, but I know there won't be anymore from him. My son is like a chihuahua around me, all bark and no bite. Besides, he's already been disrespectful, and he knows I won't tolerate it further. He discovered as much when he was a nineteen-year-old chump backtalking me. The first time, I warned him with my glare, but it ended with me throwing a steak knife at him that landed precariously close to his cock.

"Papa has a new pet. Don't you, Papa?" Rocco mocks as he spins his knife between his fingers, looking every bit the crazed man he is, but I ignore his jibes.

"You're actually fucking Robert's daughter?" Tommy asks, shock marring his features. I continue to ignore my sons and message the doctor to arrive at my house tomorrow evening. If my little pet wants a pill, she will get one, but it sure as hell won't be to prevent a pregnancy. The thought of her full of my child has my cock growing in my pants. Fuck, her tits would look impressive even fuller for me and our babies to feed on. She'd like that too, me as dependent on her as she is on me.

"Do you still manage to get it up okay, Papa?" I try not to smile at my son's taunt. If only he knew how often I do get it up. "Or do you need some of those little blue pills?"

"What will you do with her when you've had enough?" Tommy asks while Rafael continues his petulant, silent seething.

I give Tommy my attention and lift an eyebrow. "Who said I'll get enough and get rid?"

He sits forward. "You're keeping her?"

Rafael scoffs. "Another one. Great. Can we start the meeting now? We have shit to deal with."

Rocco licks his lips and tries but fails to stifle a grin. "Papa, does this one get a different color leash from the others? Because she's for keeps."

Rafael pinches the bridge of his nose. "Jesus fucking Christ," he grumbles.

Rocco's attention slices toward him. "When I took Hallie to the pet store, she picked out a nice little heart one for the puppy." His lip twitches, and Rafael's face is bordering on purple. Jesus, is my son going to have a heart attack? And he thinks he's ready for me to retire for him to take the reins?

I sit straighter in my chair and shuffle around the contracts with the O'Connell family.

A knock on the door interrupts my thoughts, and Massio opens it. "They're here."

Clearing my throat, I reply, "Another twenty." He scans the room, then his lips pull into a tight line before he nods and shuts the door.

Resting my feet on the table, I flick open the cigar box and pull out a freshly cut one placed there for me this morning, and my sons gape at me in disbelief. "A chain." I focus on Rocco, whose eyes narrow. "I won't use a leash on her like you're referring to, I will use a chain. It will feel more dominant."

Rocco's face morphs from uncertainty into jest, and I smirk at him as realization takes over his face.

"And now we have a fucking sex education lesson," Rafael complains while staring up toward the ceiling. "A depraved one at that."

"Well, I don't need any lessons." Tommy grins at his brother.

"Papa is a good tutor, taught me all kinds of shit." Rocco bounces in his seat, and not for the first time, I wonder if he should have been medicated as a child. He's always so ... wired.

I beam toward Rocco with pride. He's right, though, as unhealthy as it may sound, when my son asked for my advice, I gave it to him. After all, he didn't ask me very often, so I sure as hell wasn't turning him away when he did.

"What?" Tommy scrunches his nose; the fucker has a short memory. Pretty sure I sent him his first whore to fuck, a good one too.

All the talk about sex has my mind going back to Gracie; it's been over an hour since I saw her. I lift my phone and tap out a message.

> Me: Send me a photo of your bare pussy.

I lick my lips, waiting for her response.

> Gracie: Now?

Seeing her name light up on my phone has my heart racing. I was tempted to call her little pet in my contact list, but I like Gracie better; it feels more permanent.

> Me: Now!

My sons begin bickering about the plans for the O'Connells. Since the police commissioner has taken such an interest in our organization, they've been taking the firearms contract off us in order to deliver our shipments securely.

"What do you think, Papa?" My gaze collides with Rocco's.

"Huh?"

"I said ... What. Do. You. Think?" He speaks in the high, slow tone that pisses me off, and he damn well knows it.

DOMINATION

Rafael sighs heavily. "He's referring to the fact the O'Connells are wanting to outsource the responsibility."

I take a pull of my cigar. "Outsource." I mull over his words. "Do we know the MC they plan on using?"

Tommy sits forward. "I know them. They're legit. Reliable guys."

I consider his words.

"And you're sure Ricardo isn't involved?" I ask, wincing on his name. As much as I could throttle my absent son with my bare hands, I want none of this backfiring on him. I don't even want him to fucking know about any of it. He walked away from our life, and it wasn't until Rafael suggested he become a replacement fiancé to the girl Rocco was arranged to marry that we needed him to fulfill his destiny, and still, the little cunt acts up.

Nope, keep him the fuck out of it.

"What connection do they have to the O'Connells?" Rafael asks.

"None." Tommy's eyebrows furrow. "Not that I know of anyway."

"They will have a connection. They didn't pluck this MC out of nowhere. Do some research. We don't sign this contract with them until we know of a connection and how it benefits them," he declares, and pride takes over me at the way he's handling things.

"I'll ask around. I know a few MC guys to ask." Rocco shrugs, and I nod.

"What about asking Owen?" I throw out there.

"The man is good, but he's loyal. If he doesn't want us

to find something out, then we won't," Rafael asserts. "Leave him out of this." I nod my agreement.

My phone vibrates, and my pulse picks up, then I almost choke on the smoke of my cigar at the plush pink pussy starting back me—a swollen one, thanks to the hammering it took from me this morning.

My cock reaches toward my belt, and I have no choice but to adjust it.

> Me: Does Daddy need to kiss it better?

I lick my lips, my mouth watering to taste my cum on her sweet pussy lips.

> Me: Lick it too?

> Me: Put my tongue inside your little hole while you drip onto me.

The table rattles, and I snap my gaze up into my angry son's dark eyes. "Are you fucking listening?" Rafael looks fit to burst.

"He's sexting." Rocco's beams.

Rafael's gaze slices toward him. "What?"

Rocco motions toward my phone. "Papa, he's learned how to sext. Haven't you, Papa?"

My son's antics will be the death of me, and Rafael too, it appears. "Shut the fuck up." I reach over the table to take a swipe at his head, but he moves quicker than me, used to the threat by now.

My phone vibrates and I glance down at it.

> Gracie: Yes please, Daddy.

Jesus.

"We're fucked," Rafael throws out, and I couldn't agree more.

I'm absolutely fucked.

Chapter Thirteen

Vinny

The knock comes to the door, and I shout out for them to enter. Bren O'Connell—the O'Connell Mafia don—is followed inside by his brother Oscar. Somehow, Oscar's glower is much more abrasive than his Mafia don brother's.

"You kept us waiting," he clips out, glancing at his watch. "We've only got twenty-two minutes remaining, so I suggest you're quick."

Bren ignores his brother's snide remarks and pulls out the chair beside me while Oscar glares at my feet on the table, then opts for the chair the farthest away. It's clear the man has issues, but I've never considered analyzing them, mainly because the O'Connells are not a threat, they're allies.

"Do you always get someone else to speak for you?" I mock toward Bren.

He turns his head toward Oscar. "Oscar, shut the fuck up." Then he brings his attention back to me. "Happy?" He smirks.

Oscar looks as thrilled as Rafael did when he discovered I don't intend on letting my pet loose. Nope, the man looks like he's struggling with an internal battle. He rolls his lips and stares down at a tablet. Something he carries everywhere with him. What secrets that device must hold. Lies too, no doubt.

My phone buzzes, and I glance toward it, my fingers twitching to check if it's Gracie or not.

"Bren likes them younger too. Don't you, Bren?" Rocco smirks, and Bren glances toward the phone. Right now, I'm ready to castrate my son.

Bren simply lifts a shoulder. "Like the fact my woman hasn't had another cock." He smirks back at Rocco, whose jaw sharpens. We can agree on the fact it's satisfying to know our women are barely touched. The thought of the prick who impregnated my girl has me feral, but I remain headstrong and determined to erase all thoughts of the man from her mind and body.

I blow out a heavy, bored sigh and drop my feet to the floor, focusing on Bren and going straight for the kill. "Tell me, what are your connections with the MC?"

Bren barely blinks and glares back at me. "No connection." He lifts one of his broad shoulders, and I narrow my eyes with irritation.

"You expect me to believe that?" Fury pumps in my bloodstream at his refusal to admit they are connected. "You want us to sign a contract with an MC we know fuck all about, and you've the nerve to tell me you have no connections or dealings with them?" My voice gets louder on each word.

"Trust me. They're good people," he grunts. Good fucking people? They're a MC.

"Nineteen minutes, twelve seconds," Oscar drawls out, irritating me further, and I grind my molars so loud it's a wonder they can't hear it.

"You trust them?" I snarl back at Bren.

"Good guys." He shrugs. His lack of words is a trait of his, one that hasn't bothered me until now.

"Well, we won't be signing the contract. Get the fuck out," Rafael booms, and I want to pull my gun out to shut him up, but I try to steel my expression to remain impassive at his outburst.

Rocco glances down at his watch, then grins in Oscar's direction. "You have seventeen minutes left too, so you'll be early to your next meeting." Even I want to knock the smug smile off my son's face.

Bren and Oscar push their chairs back in unison and head toward the door. Bren throws it open while grumbling some shit under his breath, and Oscar turns his head to face me. "Robert is not to be trusted." The hairs on my neck prickle with awareness at my stepson's name on his tongue. "His daughter too." Then he walks through the door, and just like that, every limb on my body comes alive with uncertainty and at knowing I should be putting things in motion to set her free. Instead, I'm more determined than ever to dominate every inch of her. Invade every part of her until she's dependent on me: heart, body, and mind.

My little pet will be mine, and she will do exactly what her daddy commands.

Chapter Fourteen

Gracie

My day went by unbelievably slow despite being kept busy. After showering and dressing, I collected Bonnie from Hazel, then asked if it was okay to make her some breakfast, to which Hazel agreed. She even showed me where everything was and told me we can eat anything we want from the kitchen and pantry, and if they didn't have what we like, she would order it. I couldn't believe her words.

After feeding Bonnie, I bathed her and dressed her in the cute pink romper my father allowed me to purchase before coming to stay here. It looks far better on her than the dingy-looking two-piece she would usually wear at his house.

After washing our clothes from the previous day and hanging them on the chairs outside, I took Bonnie into the gardens. Vinny wasn't exaggerating when he said it was like a park out here. There's even a children's play area—I can only assume is for his grandchildren—coupled with the most luxurious swimming pool I've only ever seen on a television show, and I was in awe.

We roamed the lavish grounds, me with bare feet and Bonnie switched between crawling and being carried.

The grass is thick and green, well-watered. The flowers and shrubs are manicured, and the trees are pruned; everything is so perfect. There isn't a weed in sight, there are no old oak trees, patchy grasslands, nor fields that roam for miles. Instead, there's a wall around the perimeter with cameras, and even security guards with machine guns.

As much as I love the feeling of freedom, it still very much feels like I'm confined. And I hate it.

This is not what I want for my little girl. Still, I push the thought aside and tell myself this is so much better than being at my father's. At least here we have the means to wander at will, giving Bonnie the opportunity to thrive and develop. Here gives a sense of freedom despite there being none.

Beneath all the excitement at everything Bonnie and I discovered, I anxiously awaited Vinny's return. My eyes would dart toward the door at each sound, and when we were outside, I kept the entrances to the property in sight so I would see him at first opportunity.

Was he missing me as much as I missed him?

This is ridiculous, right? I shake my head for the hundredth time today, mentally chastising myself for being so dependent on a man I've no business depending on. My stomach rolls at the thought of not seeing him. It's been less than twelve hours, and I already feel needy. I continue to tell myself I shouldn't send him another text, not after he didn't reply to the last one.

The urge to see him borders on obsessive.

"Are you okay?" Hazel asks from over the counter.

I flick my eyes toward my phone again. "Y-yes."

She wipes her hands down her apron. "You haven't touched your sandwich." My gaze lowers toward the sandwich, and I wince.

"I'm sorry. I don't normally have lunch."

Her eyebrows shoot up into her hairline. "You don't eat lunch?"

"No." I chew on my bottom lip, wondering how much I can say without bringing more attention to myself. "I just don't feel hungry at lunchtime," I lie. Although, after spending months not eating at lunchtime, I am used to it by now.

Hazel's emerald eyes assess me, her scrutiny making me uncomfortable. When she turns toward the oven, I blow out a breath of relief and turn my attention toward Bonnie. She's been on a blanket on the floor for the past half hour, testing the selection of fresh foods I've been unable to provide her with before now.

"Do you like those, sweetie?" I stroke over her curls, and she scrunches her face into a cheeky smile that exposes her singular bottom tooth. Her happiness makes my heart soar. "Is it yummy?"

"Yu," she says while mushing the cucumber stick between her fingers.

"Good girl. Say, yum yum."

"Yu."

"Yes. Yum yum."

She mushes the cucumber into the blanket, and I wince at the mess she's creating. Hazel was kind enough to lay one down for her and told me it didn't matter since it can be washed.

"She needs a highchair," Hazel declares, then picks up her phone.

I simply nod. What else can I do? Of course she needs a highchair, she needs a stroller too, but until I can access my inheritance, I can't offer either thing.

My phone buzzes, and I spring up from the floor to grab it. Hazel chuckles and shakes her head, much like she has done all day, as if bemused by me.

Vinny is calling, and my heart races. Like an idiot, my fingers fumble with the keys, far too excited for a phone call than I should be.

"Hello?"

"Hello, Little Pet." His voice comes out smooth, but it has a dangerous edge to it I'm becoming accustomed to, addicted too almost.

"Have you eaten your lunch?"

My eyes land on my untouched plate, then slowly travel up toward Hazel and back down to the counter and her phone she's been typing on most of the day.

Has she been spying on me?

"Gracie!" Vinny barks, and I jolt.

"Have you eaten lunch?" he repeats, softer this time.

"N-no." I push my hair behind my ear. "I'm just not very hungry," I whisper.

"Little Pet, pick up your sandwich, and I want you to eat it while I speak to you. Okay?"

"Okay."

DOMINATION

"Good girl," he praises, and my body flushes with the pride in his words.

Then I smile and lift the sandwich to my mouth. If starving myself gets his attention, I know what to do in the future. I banish the thought. Besides, I have Bonnie to think about, I want to be healthy for her and set the best example I can.

"Another piece. Be Daddy's good girl and swallow it down."

A mewling sound leaves my lips.

"And another, be a good girl and lick those lips after each taste."

His husky voice sends a tremor down my spine, and I wiggle on the barstool as my panties become wetter.

Oh, dear god, I'm going to hell.

Vinny Marino can dominate every part of me any time of day.

Even lunchtime, it appears.

Chapter Fifteen

Vinny

After our meeting with the O'Connells, we head to an abandoned, rundown warehouse on the outskirts of town. One I am very aware was used to traffic women until it was shut down by the authorities.

Rafael's suggestion to use this as a location for our firearms had me concerned for his well-being, but when he pointed out that everyone involved, including the authorities who know the place is empty and practically derelict, kept a distance from the former trafficking site, I had to hand it to him, it was a great idea.

Hidden in plain sight, so to speak.

We had to remain vigilant in not bringing too much foot traffic into the warehouse so it won't raise suspicion again, but for now, it's a good location to hide our firearms while we connect the dots between the O'Connells and the relationship they have with the MC they're pushing on us.

"Your phone won't stop buzzing; it's pissing me the fuck off," Rafael sneers from the driver's seat.

Rocco sits forward from the back. "You're very tetchy today, Raf. Did mamma not give you milk this morning?" I side-eye my son. What the hell is he talking about?

Rafael's hands tighten on the steering wheel, his knuckles turning white. "Shut the fuck up, and don't mention Ellie's tits again."

Ahh, my son has a lactation kink too, it seems.

Jesus, I've created walking red flags with every kink imaginable. My lips curve, and I turn my attention out the window. The boys are so much like their father, apart from the remaining-faithful-to-one-woman part. I like far too much variety to consider tying myself down to anyone. Besides, I've never had the need to fall in love, which would be disastrous. One of us would end up with our heart broken or six feet under when an enemy discovered my weakness.

I glance at the side mirror to triple check Massio is still behind us. He's bringing Tommy's and Rafael's security details. As much as I'd like more security, it isn't a good idea; it will only force the eyes on us we're trying to avoid.

Their SUV is a reasonable distance away, and as we turn into the industrial estate, I'm relieved to see nobody is following behind.

"Papa, does Gracie call you grandpa when she fucks you?" Rocco grins, and his eyebrows dance in jest. I want to wipe the smug little fucker's smile off his face, but I refrain from doing so when my phone alerts me to another message.

DOMINATION

I smile back at the phone; Gracie sent me a photo of Bonnie eating her greens, and it's by far the cutest thing I've ever seen. She has one little tooth sticking out at the bottom, and her face is scrunched up as though she's trying to say cheese.

"You don't smile like that when I send you photos of my kids," Rocco declares, his eyebrows pinched together. He studies me, then looks down at the phone before his eyes come back to mine.

"That's because they're your children."

His face scrunches up at my lame-ass excuse. The truth is, I love my grandchildren; I delight in seeing their faces and the updates of their antics but admitting that would be too much. So, I admit that maybe I am placing some misguided love onto Gracie and her child, but it doesn't take away from the fact that I feel something for them I've never felt before.

"She's not yours." He motions toward the phone, and I grind my teeth. She may not technically be mine, but it sure as hell feels like she is, her mother too. I have the strongest urge to protect them both.

"They're mine," I state.

Rocco throws his head back on a loud obnoxious chuckle. "Fuck me. I really have got a new stepmama coming, and she's younger than me."

"Shut the fuck up," I grunt, but I can't deny the fact I like the thoughts of Gracie and Bonnie becoming permanent. I just need her on board with it too. Maybe showing her more of my lifestyle will have her invested in a future with me. If I can continue to give her the attention she craves and experience highs she's never felt before, then she will be as eager as the others to stay on.

Until I'm bored, then I will just move on to the next pet.

The thought turns my stomach.

What the hell has she done to me? She might look like an angel, but she's been sent from hell to destroy me.

Chapter Sixteen

Vinny

"Are they all there?" I drawl, watching from the only chair we have in the warehouse. I smoke my cigar, with my legs wide open as the guys check over the guns.

"They're all here," Rafael says with confidence, and I give him a nod.

"What are we going to do with him?" Tommy asks, kicking the man we have hog-tied on the floor.

The piece of shit was caught dealing in one of our clubs last night. A deal I'm pretty sure was orchestrated by Harrison Davis, the police commissioner, given the fact we were about to be raided. Thankfully, we got a heads-up, which is odd in of itself.

The kid who placed the call knew exactly who to speak to, and he knew all our names, he was familiar with us.

Odd. The whole fucking thing is odd.

"If he goes missing, you do realize they're going to know it's us," Tommy states, and I roll my eyes.

"He's already missing, dumbass," Rafael chastises, and again, my chest swells with pride at the way my son thinks so quickly on his feet. He was a born leader, through and through.

Tommy spins to face his brother. "You know what the fuck I mean."

"We gotta kill him. He's a snitch; besides, he knows too much." Rocco's eyes gleam over the point of his knife. The kid has walked around with that thing since he used it to kill one of my wives, and I couldn't agree more. We can't let him go; he knows about this place, for a start.

"Deal with him," I tell Rocco, flicking my cigar toward the man struggling against the bindings.

His screams are muffled behind the tape over his mouth, and he somehow thrashes about like a fish out of water despite him being hog-tied.

Rocco stands, towering over the man like a reaper claiming its prey. The knife glistens in his hand, and his eyes blaze with intent. "I swear my cock gets hard from this," he mumbles to himself, but I catch it, even though he insists my hearing is shit. I hear every damn word, and again, I couldn't agree more.

Every dark, sadistic, fucked-up trait my sons have are inside me too. I gave my sons a piece of my darkness, and it allowed them to create their own deranged destiny. But I'm the greatest savage of them all. People aren't aware of the depths of my sadistic needs. I only allow them to see what I want them to.

"When you're finished, leave him with me," I grunt

DOMINATION

out, and Rocco stares straight at me like he's digging into my soul, and I swear he can see everything I'm about to do. Instead of looking away from him and breaking the connection, I stare back. He licks his lips, and his chest rises.

My son might not have unlocked that part of himself yet, but when he does, I know he will be just like me.

A sadist.

Rocco has sliced and diced into the fucker's face so many times you can't tell he's human anymore; he looks like torn up meat. His fingers and hands have been removed, and the air stinks of piss and copper.

My phone vibrates in my pants pocket, and I'm torn between wanting to take it out and witness her innocence, or waiting until I leave here, as not to tarnish her image.

The feeling of anticipation is too much, so when the door closes behind my sons leaving me alone in the warehouse, I can't help myself and pull out my phone.

My heartrate kicks up, and I suck in a sharp breath as her beauty hits me square in the chest. Fuck, she's glowing. Her blonde hair appears to be blowing in the breeze, her eyes shimmer with joy, and the smile encompassing her pretty face tells me everything I need to know about how she feels.

Happiness.

A warmth spreads through me, and I quickly type out a text to her.

> Me: Go into my office, sit on my desk, push your panties to the side, and show me your bare cunt.

The three dots show up, then they disappear but start again. Annoyance flashes through me like a drug infiltrating my bloodstream. She's reluctant, I understand, but when I ask my little pet to do something, I expect a response straight away.

> Me: NOW

> Me: Don't make me punish you!

My hand clenches around the phone, and I grind my teeth.

When my phone pings again, I'm stunned speechless.

Fuck.

Her glistening pink pussy is so perfect, so small and edible, and I want to run my tongue along it, then shove it in her mouth for her to taste her little cunt from me.

Venom flows through me, and I saunter toward the remains of the man on the floor. Then I take my time unbuckling my belt and pull out my raging cock, getting lost in the thoughts of Gracie, my adorable little pet that needs fucked hard and reminded to be a good girl.

Hovering over the scum on the floor, I twist my hand, and it works faster, pumping my cock harder as my mind races with images of all the ways I would punish her for not eating her lunch.

How I'd pin her head to the mattress, mount her like

an animal, pull her asscheeks apart, then slam inside her tiny asshole while she screams at me to stop. Not giving her a chance to speak, I'd withdraw my bloody cock and slam inside her harder, faster while she cries out in pain. The frantic, controlling pace I'd put her through would give her no choice but to surrender to my demons. Her sobs would urge me on and draw my balls up, but I'd continue to hammer into her ruined ass.

My fingers clasp my cock harder, almost to the point of pain, but I embrace it, and Gracie's little cunt leaks onto the sheets, soiling them with her own secret. She likes Daddy fucking her like this. Like a whore.

Fuck yes!

I tip my head back and squeeze my eyes closed, then my cum shoots from my cock, and I aim for it to cover the dismembered torso of the fucker who dared to go against us. Images burn behind my eyes of my sweet, innocent little pet sobbing into her pillow as I come down from the ecstasy of my orgasm. My chest heaves, and I deliver the stream of piss I've been desperate to expel from my body. The degradation of the act feels so much better and more satisfying than just coming on him.

It makes me feel powerful, like he's nothing and I'm punishing him.

Gracie's parted lips flash into my mind, and I groan, then I snap my eyes open, determined not to get hard again.

When I'm finished, I shake away the remnants, tuck my cock back into my pants, and remind myself this is where I will leave my demons behind. This is where the ultimate depravity of my life remains, with the dregs of society.

My men know to clean up after me and destroy all evidence we were ever here.

I'll walk out the door and into the light to return home, and there, I will be everything I wish I was.

A better man. A caregiver. A fraud.

Her daddy.

Chapter Seventeen

Gracie

Vinny hasn't responded to the photo I sent him of me on his desk with my bare pussy out like he asked me to. I spent way too long lingering in his space than was appropriate, but his scent hanging in the air had me wishing he was there with me.

When I finally slid off his desk and sulked out of his office like a naughty schoolgirl, my face flamed at Hazel giving me a knowing smile.

Is this something he does with every woman he has a contract with? Jealousy churned my gut as I scooped Bonnie from Hazel's arms and made my way upstairs to bathe her before bed.

"Who's a pretty little princess?" I coo, and my little girl splashes in the inch of bath water. Coated in bubbles, she grins up at me and claps her hands together in glee.

A knock sounds from behind me, and as I turn, the door opens. Vinny stands against the doorframe, then his gaze wanders from Bonnie to me, and I struggle to swallow. God, he's gorgeous. His smoldering eyes travel over my body, and his jaw grinds from side to side before he somehow masks his annoyance. I fight the urge to shy away from his scrutiny, feeling inadequate for the sudden change in his demeanor.

When his gaze lifts back up to mine, he holds my stare before I glance away, dropping my hair in front of my face like a curtain, and turn my attention back to Bonnie.

"Do you have any toys?"

His question throws me off guard, and I turn to face him, blinking. Then my mind races with visions of him having an array of sex toys, and my face turns red, and I lick my lips.

A deep chuckle fills the air, and Bonnie tries to mimic him, causing us both to face her.

"Are you laughing at me, Bon-Bon?" He grins.

"Bo-Bo," she blubbers, attempting to copy his nickname for her. The fact he has one sends butterflies floating through my veins.

"Clever girl." He kneels beside the bath, then he gently tucks my hair behind my ear. "Now, when I said toys, I meant bath toys for Bonnie." He tilts his head toward the bath, and my mouth falls open. "I have plenty of those other toys, you'll find out soon enough." My eyes widen, and I try to speak but can't. "Did you bring any of her bath toys?"

My heart hammers. Partly because I'm embarrassed, stunned, and a floundering idiot, and also because she doesn't have bath toys. I clear my throat. "She doesn't have any bath toys," I state. His eyes narrow, and I worry I've said too much.

The vein on his temple throbs, and I hear him grind his teeth. My fingers itch to caress his jaw, and somehow, I find the courage to do it. The moment my hand touches his five o'clock shadow, his taut muscles relax, and he turns his cheek into my palm. "I don't know who's worse, your father or hers." His tone is solemn, and I scan his face, unsure of what he means. "Leaving her with no toys for the bath. My sons are forever sending me photos of their kids in the bath." He waves his arm out toward the tiled wall. "It looks like a fucking amusement park in their bathroom." My lip wobbles at his words, and my hand slips from his face. Being reminded what my daughter is missing out on is like a knife being plunged into my stomach. "Hey"—he brings my hand to his lips— "I'll buy her as many toys as she needs."

"She doesn't need them," I whisper. As much as I'd like my daughter to have them, they're not a necessity. I've used empty milk cartons and plastic yogurt pots for her to play with before. What's important is her future.

"I'm buying them anyway." His eyes bore into mine, most likely waiting for an argument. Finally, he clears his throat. "When you've finished bathing Bonnie, I want you bent over the bed for your punishment."

My mouth drops open. "Wh-what? Why?"

"Because I gave you an instruction, and you spoke back." He says it so casually, like he didn't just threaten me with a promise of punishment.

I rear back. "Is that in the contract?"

He eyes me with suspicion, and I instantly find the

hem of my T-shirt to cling onto. His eyes travel over me, and once again, I find myself feeling inadequate. "I don't know. Is it?" His eyes have darkened, and my throat becomes dry as he challenges me.

"I-I haven't gotten around to reading it all yet."

He sighs heavily, and I hate the way his face falls with disappointment. I want to throw my arms around his neck and beg him for my forgiveness, which is just ridiculous, but I long to have his reassurance. I blink back the tears threatening to spill, and when his warm hand cups my chin and turns my head to face him, I let out a sigh of relief that his face is no longer etched in sorrow. "Do you want me to bathe you?" His husky voice sends a shot of enthusiasm through me, and I nod.

He glances back toward Bonnie. "Will she need fed before she goes to sleep?"

"Probably."

He nods. "I have a doctor coming over to give you your birth control shot." My heart leaps in my chest. "But first, I have some calls to make. I want you to get Bon-Bon"—my breathing stutters again at his nickname—"ready for bed, feed her, then put her down for bedtime."

"What about my bath?" I ask, and his lip curls into a smile.

"I'll bathe with you once the doctor has finished."

I nod, a thrill of excitement zipping up my spine, and when he leans forward and places his lips on my forehead, I melt beneath his touch, and between my legs becomes wet.

"Good girl," he rasps, probably knowing the effect he has on me.

DOMINATION

I don't think he realizes the depths of my desire for him, and my feelings are the scariest part. If he wanted me to stay forever, I'd throw my plan out the window to keep him.

But I can't do that, not with our lives at stake.

Chapter Eighteen

Vinny

"Tell me everything," I bite out before Hazel has even closed the office door. She opens her mouth to speak, but I beat her to it. "Message after fucking message all day long." I rub my temple; I'm getting too damn old for all this shit.

"You said to let you know of everything she does and any suspicions," she counters, and she's right, I did.

"Tell me everything, from the start." I roll my hand for her to start speaking.

"Well—" She takes a deep breath, then helps herself to a chair at my desk without so much as asking. Anticipation buzzes through me, and I want to put a gun to her head and tell her to get the fuck on with it, but I remember who she is and what I asked of her. Her direct instructions were to tell me everything and anything about Gracie, but I didn't expect a running commentary about their day. Despite enjoying it, the moment red flags were raised, I wanted to get back home to her and demand answers, but my little pet is skittish. She longs for reassurance and comfort, and her big blue eyes plead for tenderness. Yet another reason I can't ever reveal my true self to her. She'd hate me, and I can't have that—it would destroy anything good I have left in me.

Hazel glances around the room like she hasn't been in here a million times.

Annoyance bubbles inside me. "Hazel?"

"Hmm?"

"What the fuck have you learned?" I grit out, trying but failing to rein in my temper.

She flinches, then sits taller. "Oh. Well, it was very odd this morning when she handwashed hers and the baby's clothes, then she dried them outside. I don't think they have many."

"Many what?" I narrow my eyes on her. "Many what, Hazel?" I bark out.

"Clothes." Her eyes bore into mine as if I'm an idiot.

Taking a deep breath, I sit back in my chair and shake my head. That can't be right. I send enough money to her father every month, so he should be able to care for them all. Then I think back to the comment in the bathroom about the lack of bath toys for Bonnie.

"And little Bonnie. She doesn't have much at all." Hazel clucks her tongue, and her words send a rush of fury through me.

My spine snaps straight, and I lean forward. If she didn't know better, my glare alone would have her pissing her pants. "What do you mean she doesn't have much?"

DOMINATION

She nods frantically, then starts marking things off on her fingers. "No highchair, no stroller, no real toys, just a pink stuffie. No throw away diapers, they're the washable ones, and to be honest, they look brand new, like they were recently purchased. Gracie made a comment that Bonnie's dress and bow was new for dinner with you, and I think those diapers are too."

Pure rage slithers through me, but Hazel isn't remotely fazed as she goes on. "I don't think they have much at all, and Gracie was delighted she could feed Bonnie new foods. She acted like a cucumber was a new food to offer Bonnie." She scoffs, and I feel like I'm having an out-of-body experience as my blood boils like lava.

"A cucumber?" I force the word out like poison. How fucking ludicrous. That little angel should be having a balanced diet, full of natural goodness and nutrients every day of her goddamn life, and I expect as much for how much money I throw that little punk's way.

I'm feeling fucking murderous. "I want a dietitian to take a look at them both."

"I was going to suggest that, so I researched the best in the area. If you could just get Massio to double-check." Hazel leans forward and hands me the piece of paper. I could kiss the woman, but instead, I grunt my gratitude.

The need to wrap my hands around Robert's throat and strangle the life out of him has never been so strong.

"She hasn't read the contract yet," I muse, dragging a finger over my bottom lip.

Hazel makes a tsking noise and shakes her head. "Silly girl. She could have signed her life away, hers and her daughters. You need to be putting her straight, she needs to be much more alert and thorough in the future."

"Her future's with me," I state.

A smile creeps over her face, then she leans across the desk and pats my hand like I'm a child and not a sick fuck who likes to jerk off over dead bodies, imagining it's a woman I've terrorized. "Pleased to hear it." She beams, then stands.

A knock at the door alerts me to the fact the doctor has more than likely arrived. "Yeah?"

Massio enters and leads our family doctor into the office while Hazel slinks out of the room and closes the door behind her. I slide the name and number of the dietitian across my desk and tap it. "Have you heard of this man?"

Doctor Philips pushes his glasses up his nose, then nods. "He's one of the best."

I glance toward Massio. "Check him out and then organize a visit for Gracie and Bonnie."

"Yes, sir."

"You"—I point toward the man who delivered my sons—"I want her pregnant as soon as possible."

"Y-yes sir."

"I don't give a shit what you must give her; I'll do my part and pump her with enough cum her body won't have a choice but to accept it. Assuming you do your bit, she will be with child in no time." I sit back in my chair, and he scratches his head.

"Sir, if I could just say?"

My teeth grind on their own accord. I'm not going to

like what he's about to say, based on the fact he's fidgeting so damn much, sweating like a pope in a whore house, and is struggling to give me eye contact.

"What?" I snipe out so loud even Massio flinches.

He clears his throat. "You're much older than when you had your last child." Fury engulfs me like a red haze, but he continues. "What I mean is, yo-your sperm might not be as fertile."

I scoff. "Of course it fucking is. I need to come a lot." I waft my hand. If that's his concern, it's pointless.

"Sir?" He clears his throat.

"That doesn't necessarily mean it's fertile."

"I am," I state, "very fucking fertile. Now do your job and get her up to speed too."

"You said she has a baby?"

"Yes, a daughter."

"Well, if the baby is below a year, she's probably highly fertile herself."

My muscles relax and I exhale. "Good. I will have you return in a few weeks to see if she's pregnant." The thought of my child growing inside her has an overwhelming sense of pride and possession ravishing me. My body comes alive, and a sense of hope I haven't felt before surges through me. My mind wanders, and I imagine trailing my hand over her soft skin and my palm encompassing her small bump, how I'll dote on her as she deserves, make her my queen, and tend to her every need.

"Sir?" Massio pulls me out of my thoughts, and I adjust my cock, uncaring if either of them witnesses it, causing him to laugh at my action. "You wanna get this over with?" He throws his thumb toward the doc, and I nod. He's right, the sooner I have her injected, the sooner she becomes mine forever.

Chapter Nineteen

Vinny

I pinch the bridge of my nose.
"B-but I want the pill. I don't like injections." Gracie paces the room like a wildcat while tugging on her hair.

"It says in the contract you will receive birth control via a syringe, Gracie," I snipe out.

She spins to face me. "I don't like injections. I'll take the pill." Her bottom lip quivers, and I almost give in, almost. I mean, surely, there's something he can give her orally. Then again, I want this sorted today, now. "I swear I'll take it. I'll show you every day."

My jaw locks up tight, and I shake my head.

"Ahhh!" she screams like a banshee, and I swear my ear drums are damaged now, something Rocco will be amused with.

"You're acting like a brat," I chastise from the chair in the corner of her bedroom, watching her unravel. She's now got her head in her hands, tugging on her luscious locks.

I glance toward Doctor Philips, and the chump is dabbing his forehead with a handkerchief.

"Come here," I demand, pointing at the floor between my feet, then lean back in my chair, with my elbows resting on the arms.

A tension builds between us, with her glaring back at me. Her chest heaves, then she glances toward the doctor, pissing me off further. Anger coils inside me at her defiance, but I refuse to show it; she needs comfort not anger. "Gracie! Come." I point again, and defeat floods her face. Conscious of upsetting her further, I soften my tone. "Come, Little Pet," I croon, holding my hand out for her.

She shuffles toward me, with tears pooling in her eyes, and the moment she's within reach, I tug her to me until her chest collides with mine. Then I yank on the ring of her collar. "Unzip me, and use me while I take care of you." I stroke her hair, and she turns into my palm.

Releasing the ring, I take her face into the palms of my thick hands and swipe away her tears as our eyes remain transfixed on one another. "Stop crying. I don't like it when you cry, Little Pet." She sniffles and nods. "Daddy's going to put his cock inside you as soon as the doctor's gone." She licks her lips, and my cock jumps in my pants. "I'm going to let you suck me while you let the doctor do his job." Her lip wobbles, and I lean forward and kiss it, loving the way her fingernails dig into my skin beneath my shirt. She's worked up and acting out, like a feral animal that needs reminded of who its owner is yet needing taken care of too. "Are you wearing any panties?" I rasp in her ear while I finger over the lace of her sleep shorts.

"Yes."

"The contract says you're not to wear panties at night."

"Oh."

Oh? Is she serious? Frustration has me growling, but I banish it when her eyes flash with disappointment. I stroke over her golden locks and down her spine. A small shudder escapes her, and she leans into me. "Good girl." One of her arms remains banded around my neck, and she nuzzles against my chest.

Once she's content with my handling of her, I push on her shoulders, and she slides to the floor. When I rest back in the chair and widen my legs, she takes it as her cue to unbuckle me. Her small fingers tremble as she pops open my pants and slowly lowers my zipper.

Arousal has my heart beating rapidly, and when her soft hand slips into my boxers, my eyes roll and I hiss out a breath of exhilaration.

She tugs my boxers down, and her small mouth encompasses the head of my cock. She almost strangles my cock with her grip while frantically sucking on the head, and the urge to remain controlled is driving me wild.

Caressing her head, I relish the silkiness of her locks. "Take your time, Little Pet. Let Daddy care for you."

Her eager sucking lessens, and I deliver an array of praise to her. "You're doing so well sucking on me." Her tongue swipes over the tip, causing me to jolt at the sensation that rips up my spine. "Such a good little pet." The vibration of her moan has me gritting my teeth. "So beautiful. The prettiest little pet." Her hand eases around me, and her sucking has become rhythmic as she uses me for comfort. I take this opportunity to meet the doc's eyes and lift my chin. I'm grateful for the way he keeps the needle hidden as he approaches her. She stiffens, no doubt hearing his footsteps, and I want to gut the fucker for causing her unease. The glare I throw him is venomous, and he darts his eyes away from mine as he towers above her. "Get it over with," I snipe out.

A small whimper leaves her, and her nails bite into my thigh, bound to leave crescent marks I will wear with pride. Her lips work faster as he brings the needle toward her. I know the exact moment he injects her because her small body stiffens, her teeth scrape along my flesh, and a strangled cry escapes her. I welcome the bite of pain, and beads of pre-cum spill from the tip of my cock. "That's it, use your daddy, take what you need." I hold her head against my groin, and she whimpers, her warm breath fanning over me. "Shh, it's okay Gracie, it's okay," I soothe, continuing to coddle her. My little pet needs reassurance, and reassurance she will have.

It's over quickly, and I glare toward the doc. He swallows hard, then backs away from us, grabs his bag, and heads out of the room.

I lift my angel into my arms, cradling her against me, and breathe in her scent. Lowering her on to the mattress, she doesn't so much as flinch, almost like she's in shock. Over a fucking needle.

I peer down at her, cracking my neck from side to

side to ease the tension. It's been one hell of a day. Languorously, I unbutton my shirt and kick my pants and boxers to the floor while my gaze darkens on the little beauty in my bed. The moment I wrap my fist around my cock, I know I won't last long. I kneel on the end of the mattress, grab a hold of her legs, and yank her to the edge to slide down her sleep shorts and panties.

My muscles pull tight as my cock drips pre-cum. "Fuck," I hiss, and my free hand slides over her silky, smooth skin. "You're so fucking perfect, and you don't even know it," I coo. I slap my cock against her slick entrance, and she clenches, it's like she's waiting for me to fill. "It's okay, Little Pet, Daddy's here." Then I repeat the motion, relishing the slapping sound before I slide inside her.

Electricity shoots up my spine when her warm heat grips me, and I thrust forward to the hilt. A whimper escapes her lips, and an intense pleasure zips up my spine. After pulling out, I slam forward, loving the way her compliant body welcomes me with each thrust. My grip on her thigh tightens, and I know it will bruise, but I don't care, I'll tend to it after. Me.

The way her pussy molds to my cock is an aphrodisiac. I'm completely obsessed with her. She's my kryptonite, my fucking everything. I've never felt like this before, ever. I've never wanted to be so deep inside someone I don't want to leave, and I tell myself it's because I'm the only one to have entered her, though I know otherwise. I want to keep her, breed her, and feed from her tits as her body swells with our baby.

Removing my hand from her thigh, I spit onto her

pussy, causing my cock to jump at the sight. When I circle her little clit, a small moan leaves her pouty lips, and I flick my eyes up to watch the way her tits bounce with each movement. Each powerful surge has me moving closer and closer toward my orgasm. Her body convulses, her pussy clenching my cock hard. "Fuck," I grit out. "That's it, Little Pet, breed for Daddy." Warm cum spurts into her, and I close my eyes, willing my seed to ensure our future together.

Chapter Twenty

Gracie

Vinny is thorough as he washes me. I lean back against his strong chest, sinking into him for comfort—the thump of his heart beating against me is soothing. He's powerful and demanding, forceful and controlling, but above all else, he's caring and tender, and I crave that part of him as much as all the others.

The bath is full of bubbles and smells of peaches, and I smile when he nuzzles into my neck and places another feathery kiss just below my ear and the bite marks he's created over the past few days.

His hands work the suds down my body, and I delight in the way his hard cock flinches when he kisses me, as if he's struggling to hold back his need. The cleansing of me becomes more of a massage, and I'm grateful for his touch.

"Why don't you like needles?"

My blood turns to ice, and I freeze, and his voice

turns deadly. "Little Pet?" he murmurs when I don't answer right away.

"I-I just don't."

He tsks under his breath, and his arm crosses over my chest until his hand wraps loosely around my throat. It's not in the least bit threatening, more of a commanding action. "I asked you why you don't like needles. Answer."

"When I first moved in with him, my father's friends used them, and I didn't like what they did to them."

A small shudder racks through him, and his fingertips tighten. "What did they do, Little Pet?"

"They used them for drugs, and they—" My throat clogs and I still, unable to admit the part I hate the most.

He kisses the top of my head and nuzzles into my hair, all while holding my throat captive under his command. "Go on."

"My father injected me to make me go to sleep." My heart booms behind my rib cage. "But he hasn't since I became pregnant," I rush out.

His muscles tighten and his body stiffens before he drops his hands to his side, causing the water to splash over the tub. My shoulders sag, the familiar feeling of abandonment I've become accustomed to rears its ugly head, and tears build behind my eyes.

"Shhh, Little Pet," he coos, and wraps his arms around my center. "Daddy's here." Then he clears his throat. "Why did he want you to go to sleep, Gracie?"

I revel in the way he uses my nickname and my given name, so easily flipping between the two. I can't help but wonder if this is usual practice for him or if he only uses the term little pet for his usual women.

DOMINATION

Jealousy creeps up my spine, but I shake it away, choosing to concentrate on the here and now while believing he doesn't so much as know anyone else's given name. Glancing down at the firm embrace he has on me, I use the tip of my finger to the follow the veins running from his hand and over his thick arms, wishing it was my tongue traveling over him with the same confidence.

I tilt my head up to face him. "He said I had to be quiet and not see."

His silver eyebrows furrow. "Not see what?"

I think on his question for a minute. Truth be told, I'm unsure, but I've always assumed he meant he didn't want me to witness his dealings. "The men that were coming to do drugs and things."

"Good girl," he praises, and I smile. "He won't be injecting you again." His tone is forceful and deadly. "I'm proud you let me look after you so you could have your shot."

I nod at his words, grateful he understands the enormity of my phobia. His thick hand spans my stomach, and butterflies swirl inside me.

"How I wish my hand was resting here when you were pregnant." He laughs, and my blood stills, my heart stutters, and I suck in a sharp breath.

He nips at my ear and pushes his hard cock into my back. "You're a good girl, letting Daddy breed you, Little Pet."

My eyebrows furrow, and I tilt my head back to question him. "I'm on birth control now."

He chuckles, causing his chest to vibrate and my tits to bounce. His focus moves to them, and he licks his lips before his darkened eyes lock back on mine. "I know. But I can still try and fuck you until I make you swell."

This time, it's me who giggles, and I find myself squeezing my legs together at how he would be if I was pregnant.

His hands move over my stomach, encompassing it. "I'd like to see this belly full of my baby."

My breath hitches as moisture gathers between my legs. "You would?"

Another kiss is placed below my ear. "I'd like to fuck your little cunt while you grow what's mine. Palm your stomach while I fuck into you. Suck on your tits and drink my milk while you plead with me to keep you pregnant." He palms my breasts in his thick hands and flicks my nipples, causing my back to arch into his touch. "To feel my baby move inside you while I suckle on the milk you provide for us." Then he sucks my neck, and I cry out as an orgasm is ripped from me.

Chapter Twenty-One

Vinny

Hearing Gracie describe how that piece of shit would inject her while he dealt in shit he had no reason dealing in, infuriates me. The only saving grace in that conversation is that he didn't continue to drug her while she was pregnant.

Still, the man will suffer for involving an innocent girl in his misdeeds.

Even if she wanted to move back in with her father, there's no way that is happening now.

My angel is spread out on my bed on a towel, and I spend my time drying her. When I tap her thigh, she opens her legs, and I chuckle at the blush creeping over her face and down her chest.

Her puffy pink pussy lips are glistening with arousal, and I lick my lips, but instead of tasting her, I ignore the way my cock peeks out of the towel wrapped around my waist, desperate to get in on the action, and dab her little pussy with the towel to dry her. Then I lift her leg into the air to expose her little asshole. Fuck, that looks inviting. When I press the towel to her to wipe away the droplets of water, my solid cock leaks pre-cum over my abs, leaving me a sticky mess as I continue to dry her with tenderness.

She watches from the bed, and I unwrap the towel from around my waist. Her bright-blue eyes have darkened, and she licks her lips in a manner that tells me she has no clue she's even doing it. I curl my fist around my length and pump my cock a couple times, delighting in the stream of pre-cum dripping down my fist. Then I move around the bed and position myself so my head is resting on the pillow beside her. Her eyes haven't left mine, so beautifully submissive for me and awaiting my instruction.

I take a lock of her hair between my fingers, toying with the silkiness as I tell her what I want. "I want you to climb on my face and rub your sweet little pussy over my beard, then you're going to ride me until you come all over my lips, Little Pet. I want to taste your pussy juice all over my face. I want to drink down your pleasure."

Her breath hitches and her blush deepens, and when she chews into her bottom lip like she is contemplating her next move, I almost combust. Frankly, she doesn't have a choice. Instead of telling her this, I lift her by her hips, causing a little squeak to leave her. I can't help but think she's so damn tiny and light compared to the other women I've fucked; another reason she needs my protection and I can't let her go.

I position her lithe body so she's straddling my head,

then grip her asscheeks and tug her lower. "Rub your pussy on me," I command, and her pupils flare as I rock her back and forth over the bristle of my whiskers.

"Oh, god, Daddy," she pants, and her hands find the headboard to help stabilize her.

I shake my head. "Your tits, baby. Play with your tits. I want your milk to flow down and splash on my face while you fuck me." My cock jumps in response to my filthy words. "Fucking drench me in your milk," I bite out.

Her hands move to massage her tits. "Like this, Daddy?"

My eyes roll at the sight. Milk bubbles from her nipples and spills over the tips of her fingers. "Fuck yes," I grind out.

She presses her pussy down on my mouth, and I suck at her folds, lick at her slit, and devour her pussy hole with each movement. "Mm, Daddy. Oh, god."

My balls ache at the most beautiful sight—watching my girl chase her orgasm with little prompting, and she takes it upon herself to ride my face like a little slut. "Keep fucking my face, Little Pet. Keep taking what you need like a slutty little girl."

"Daddy, I'm covering you in milk," she pants, yet continues to ride me, grinding down on my mouth with each movement.

Milk rolls down her stomach and over my face as her breathing escalates. "Good. Good girl."

My tongue laps at her, and my eyes roll at imagining taking her face freely like she's taking mine. I never let loose on a woman how I'd like to, too afraid to scare them away when I enjoy the tenderness as much as the abrasiveness, a contradiction if ever there was one. Instead, I remain controlled, but with the sounds of pleasure emanating from my little pet, I've never come so close to delving into my darkness and using someone for my depravity. I want to own every inch of her, in every way of my choosing, but the last thing I want to do is terrify my innocent little pet and have her look at me differently. I don't want her to see me as anything other than her everything, the man who protects and cares for her.

The man who is her daddy.

"Oh, god. Oh, god, Daddy. I-I'm ..." She throws her head back, and her body coils tightly.

"That's it, Little Pet," I croon, stroking the globes of her toned ass. "Come all over your daddy."

Chapter Twenty-Two

Vinny

The sound of my alarm has me reaching out and fumbling to swipe the alert from my cellphone. "Fuck," I grunt, mentally running through the day ahead of me. I'm getting too damn old for these early starts and long days. Having to always be mentally and physically on point is draining, and while my body is slowing down, it appears my mind wants to too.

The soft suckling of her lips pulls me from my thoughts, and I lift the bed sheet to glance down at her. Her bright-blue eyes meet mine, so I throw the sheet back and drop my head against my pillow to watch her. My fingers tangle in her silky locks while she suckles on my cock, causing it to harden. The last thing I want is for her to make me come. I enjoy the pleasure of simply watching my pets suckle on me like I provide comfort for them. This isn't sexual gratification in the usual sense, but

I sure as fuck get gratification knowing my body is bringing them solitude.

She removes her mouth from my cock, making a popping sound that has my balls tightening. Fuck, she's incredible.

After she fucked my face last night, I filled her little pussy with my cum while her tits bounced in my face and I drank her milk.

I lift a handful of her hair and let it slip between my fingers. "I'm going to leave you my black card today, I want you to go shopping."

She frowns and stares back at me. "I don't need anything."

Annoyance rumbles in my chest, but I try my best to remain impassive. "Yes, you do."

Her lips twist. "Like what?"

"Clothes, Gracie, for you and Bonnie," I snap, and throw my legs over the edge of the bed. Groaning, I rub my head before wincing at the aches radiating from me, courtesy of the Mafia lifestyle.

I don't have time for her petulance today, but that doesn't mean I won't punish her for it later.

"We have clothes!" she shouts as I open the bathroom door, so I glance over my shoulder, locking eyes with hers, and my heart skips a beat. Why the fuck do I have these reactions toward her? She's far too young for an old man like me.

"Then buy more!" I bellow, stepping into the bathroom, then slam the door behind me. What the fuck is wrong with her? Any other woman would snatch my hand off and suck me dry for offering a black card to them. Hell, she didn't even ask if she had a budget.

Twenty minutes later, I'm showered, dressed, and heading into the kitchen. I flip the cap on my morning smoothie and drink it down. Then, without missing a beat, I power on the coffee machine and place a freshly baked croissant on my plate along with the small dish of butter and jelly.

Glancing down at my phone, I shoot my sons a message in our group chat.

> Me: ETA, eight a.m.

> Tommy: Seriously? I've been up all night with teething babies.

A smile crosses my face. The thought of Tommy in a domestic lifestyle with his once stepdaughter is a far cry from the man who couldn't keep up with escorts he had on a nightly basis. I thank my lucky stars every damn day that his stepdaughter, Jade, was mistaken for one of them.

> Rafael: I've been ready since seven.

> Rocco: Well done, you. Pretty sure Papa has incontinence issues, so he wet the bed, am I right?

The little shit sets my teeth on edge.

> Me: The only bed wetting is my girl's pussy drenching the sheets.

> Rafael: Too much information. Not to mention, that girl is your granddaughter.

A smirk spreads over my face. The taboo aspect of our relationship is quite the turn-on, I admit.

> Rocco: I bet Papa likes watersports too, am I right?

I drag a finger over my trimmed beard. He's not wrong, and yet another sign my son's depravity might be inherited, otherwise, there's no other explanation for it.

> Tommy: You pay way too much attention to what Papa does.

> Me: He's learned from the best.

I can practically see Rafael's eyes roll as he reads that.

> Rafael: The last thing I want is my children knowing I piss on their mama.

Here he fucking goes; the little pricks love to remind me I exploited my sexual preferences in front of them. Something else I would change if I could go back. Though I don't recall pissing on any of my pets or wives in their presence. My jaw tics and my hands ball into fists. I should have been more vigilant, more of a father. I love my boys more than anything, but Mafia life took over so much I never gave them the childhood they deserved, and if I could go back in time, I wouldn't change it. They became the best versions of themselves that they need to be to survive this world.

DOMINATION

It doesn't mean I have to like it or that I'm proud of all my actions.

> Rocco: I missed seeing that.

There, confirmation I never did it in front of my kids. The tension eases from me as I exhale a breath I wasn't aware I was holding.

> Rafael: It was the one that tried to drown you.

Fan-fucking-tastic.

I'm a useless father. No wonder I prefer to shower women in affection. I never get this hassle from them. I leave the phone on the counter, then grab the tray and kick open the door to the breakfast room.

I freeze. *Holy fuck!*

There she is, naked and kneeling for me, and all thoughts of being pissed at my sons and punishing her for her attitude are banished.

The moment I slip onto my chair and shuffle forward, her hands move to rest on my thighs, and I stroke her hair. "Good Little Pet."

She lifts her head, and the emotion in her eyes stuns me for a second. "I want you to be happy with me."

My breath catches. Does she seriously think I could be anything other than happy with her? Does she think I won't keep her if she doesn't behave?

"Daddy is very happy with you." I smooth over her hair as she works my zipper down, and suddenly, my day feels a whole lot better.

175

Chapter Twenty-Three

Gracie

Hazel is babysitting for me, and to say it feels strange to be out of the house without Bonnie is an understatement. I don't like it. Add in the fact I've never been to a mall before, and every sight and sound leaves my pulse racing as my gaze flicks from one store to the next.

The marbled floors and high ceilings with extravagant lighting are not how I envisaged a mall to be. The shops have elegant dresses in the windows; some have gold lettering above the doors, and others have fancy entrances to entice you. Each makes me feel out of my element. I do not belong here, not at all.

"Can I suggest actually going in a store?" Massio drawls, pointing toward one of the stores. He's clearly agitated he's been left to escort me. The way he watches me with contempt has my nerves on edge, but I never asked for a bodyguard.

"I-I don't know which one to go in," I admit, hating the sound of my own voice.

He sighs heavily, then drags his hand over his shaved head. If he wasn't such an ass, he'd be handsome, but that coupled with the fact he doesn't have silver streaks in his hair, wrinkles around his eyes, or slightly weathered skin has me cringing. I'm pretty sure he feels the same way about me, given how he tends to look through me instead of at me.

"Boss said you need clothes. The women he uses tend to come back with bags from in there." He points toward a boutique, but my spine bolts straight and anger radiates through me. I don't want to be one of them. I don't want to be another pet that gets used and disposed of, to dress and act like them.

Is that what he thinks of me? Is he trying to mold me into one of those women?

I lift my chin high. "I'll find my own store."

He chuckles, and his eyes dance with humor, then he glances at his watch. "Can you hurry up? I'd like to do some real work today."

"You're an ass," I snap, and march toward a store that looks more like a thrift store than a boutique and out of place in the glamorous mall.

After trudging through the endless shops, we finally make it back to Vinny's house. I want nothing more than to refer to it as my home, but it isn't and if I'm honest, the constraints of the Mafia lifestyle never will be, not when my heart is at the ranch. My home is nestled among the fields, where freedom lies in wait. Where Bonnie can grow up without threats of violence and bloodshed, without manipulation and cruelty.

Just me and her.

I rub at the sting in my chest at considering being without Vinny, the one man who has somehow grasped my heart in the palms of his thick hands and cradled it to the point of awe and affection.

Only, I know it's going be ripped from his hands and destroyed. By my own doing, no less.

The moment Bonnie's squeal of delight fills my ears, my heart swells. This is why I'm here, it was never my choice.

It was all stolen from me the moment I agreed to the arrangement with my father.

Two years ago...

"Up!" He lifts me by my elbow, and my legs buckle. So weak from the lack of food I can barely stand, but somehow, I shuffle behind him and up the stairs from the basement. My feet are numb from the cold, and each step I take feels like a heavy weight pulling me down.

The warmth of his small home hits me, and I wince at the sun streaming through the kitchen windows. Garbage is stacked on the counter, and the scent of the discarded half pizza has my stomach rumbling.

A sadistic chuckle leaves him, and I cower, which only causes his grip on me to tighten. Then he pushes me into one of the kitchen chairs while he takes the other one beside me.

Slowly, I take in my surroundings. Unable to remember the last time I came up here, I look for something different than before but find nothing. It's all the same. A shithole.

Empty bottles of alcohol are strewn across the floor, the trash is spilled over, and drug paraphernalia coats the arms of the disused sofa. The needle on the floor causes my stomach to roll like a cruel taunt. Whenever I don't comply, he uses a needle on me, and I hate it. I hate the way my blood curdles and sickness lodges in my throat, the way my body sways and is unwilling to move at my instruction. I hate needles, and mostly, I hate him.

"Here's what's going to happen." He pushes a stack of papers in my direction. "You're almost eighteen now." I nod, knowing I'm almost old enough to be out of his evil clutches. "My stepfather, Vincent Marino, has an annual Halloween party." I nod again, remembering the venom that spilled from my father's lips whenever he discussed his stepfather and his family. "You're going to go to that party, and you're going to whore yourself out to this man." He taps the photo on the paperwork. As I look down into the dark eyes of the handsome man, I feel like my soul is being snatched from me. The good girl I prided myself on being will be ripped away. I've never had sex before, not for any reason, but I've never had the opportunity, never met someone I've wanted to do it with.

Could I with this man?

I glance down at the papers, chewing on my lip, and trace his broad shoulders with my finger. "Who is he?" My scratchy voice comes out on a whisper.

"Your grandfather." My gaze snaps up toward his, and a menacing smile plays on his lips. "You're about to seduce your grandfather, Gracie, and in return, you get your life back." His smile grows wider as he flips the page to what looks like dozens of legal documents. Hope springs in my chest, and he thrusts a pen into the palm of my hand

before curling his fingers around mine so tightly the pen digs into my skin.

"I just need your compliance as insurance, then we both get what we want."

Only, I never got what I wanted. Not yet at least. But I will. More determined than ever before.

Vinny

My focus isn't on the meeting. It isn't on the fact Rocco and Rafael have made progress with building a connection with the MC affiliated with the O'Connells. Nope, it's on my little pet. The girl who has swooped in and captured my attention and, worse, my heart.

Massio had the privilege of taking her shopping this morning, much to his dissatisfaction. In fact, his lip curled into a sneer before he cleared his throat and grunted his approval when I cocked an eyebrow to his objection.

I messaged him frequently throughout the day, eager to know of her progress. Despite Massio assuring me there'd been none, I knew he was fucking with me. No woman goes to a mall with a black card and returns unhappy or leaves emptyhanded.

When Rafael declared he was making moves to shake up the drug dealers who dared enter our club last night, I feigned boredom at his suggestions and told him and Rocco to go ahead without me. I had security drive me home because, like an addict, I was craving the only thing that could appease me—her.

Maybe I'm more like my stepson than I care to believe. Maybe Tommy's addictions were of my doing too. Another parenting fuck-up of mine, yet I still drive into Gracie at every opportunity, knowing I'm fucking her bareback. Am I really that desperate to keep her that I'd risk having another child at my age? My cock twitches in glee, and when a wooden spoon clocks me on the side of my head, I'm pulled from my thoughts and reminded of the present.

"Bon-Bon, seriously? No hitting Papa," I chastise in a playful tone I only remember using on my grandchildren.

The house feels somewhat empty without Gracie being here, and I check my phone again, tracking the car returning to the house. Until she walks through the door, I will remain on edge. Sending her shopping without me was not a good idea. Massio might be the best man I know to protect her, but that didn't help with the ball of dread as she left.

It was one of the reasons I insisted on Hazel babysitting Bonnie—so I knew she'd return.

She giggles loudly, causing her chubby tummy to bounce. "Pa!" She shocks the shit out of me, then whacks me with the spoon again. "Pa!" she says louder, exposing her bottom teeth and making me grin from ear to ear. She's the cutest little baby I've seen, a mirror image of her momma, and jealousy creeps into my bloodstream at the thought of someone else giving her the greatest gift. Someone stole that from me.

The darkness inside me rears its ugly head, and I

suddenly want to track the fucker down and dismember him for taking what should have been mine.

The sooner she's pregnant with my child, the better. Yes, a replica of my perfect little Bon-Bon.

"Papa!" Bonnie declares, pushing up from the floor and using her chubby hands to stand.

The sound of her calling me the same name my sons call me has my lungs constricting, and I hold my hands to her. "Come on. Come to Papa," I coax. She grins a drooly grin, and as she steps toward me, a surge of excitement swells in my chest. "Come on, Bon-Bon," I urge. "You can do it!"

She sways on her feet but somehow stays upright, and when she takes the two steps toward me, I catch her as she falls into my arms. "Clever girl." I deliver soft kisses on her nest of curls. "Such a clever girl for Papa." I smile and shower her in praise.

A gasp of surprise pulls my attention toward the door. "She took her first steps?" Gracie steps into the room.

"She did." I maneuver her onto my hip and stand. "Did you see?" I beam back at Gracie.

Tears have filled her eyes. "Yes! She walked to you."

I pull her toward me to have both my girls nestled against my chest. Bonnie plays with the buttons on my shirt, and I place a kiss on top of her momma's head and breathe in her peach scent to help settle the anxiety from her absence.

"I can't believe she walked for you." Awe laces her tone, and pride fills my bloodstream. I don't ever recall watching the boys walk for me, and truth be told, I'm not sure I would've even given a fuck. I had men to slay, a reputation to uphold, and a literal bloodbath on my doorstep to conceal from their eyes. The last thing I had time for was my children.

A knock sounds from the doorway, and Massio steps inside, something I will have to discuss with him. While the other women I paraded around the mansion with little to no thought, I don't want him seeing Gracie in a state of undress. "Sir?"

"What?" I snap, and he rears back like I punched him in the gut.

He swallows thickly. "You asked for an update?"

He's referring to Gracie and the day they spent together, a day she should have spent with me. Did he watch her as she tried clothes on? Does he know what she bought? Again, jealousy slivers through my veins, and my body stiffens, but I shove the foreign feelings aside and place Bonnie in her momma's arms while twirling the hook of her collar around as a reminder of who she belongs to. "She will want to eat soon. Save me some." I speak low, for only her ears, and delight in the way she nods, then I step past her and follow Massio into my office.

The moment the door closes behind him, I head toward the decanter and pour us both two fingers of whiskey. I place the glass down in front of him and nurse mine, then settle my old ass on my chair. "Go on," I prompt.

"She didn't buy a damn thing for herself. You made me traipse around all those fucking stores, and she didn't buy anything for her." He shakes his head, and his lips twist in disgust. If I was anything but pissed right now, I'd find his reaction amusing, but who the hell has she been buying things for?

"She bought the baby half a dozen things: clothes, a bath toy, blanket etc." He wafts his hand and takes a swig of his whiskey. "Then she bought you this." A smug smile spreads across his face as he digs into his jacket pocket to retrieve a small bag that he then hands to me. When I remove the black material from inside, I frown.

"A tie, to match your eyes apparently." He scoffs and rolls his eyes, and the jest in his tone pisses me off. "More like to match your fucking soul." That makes my lips twitch, but anger still simmers in my bloodstream at the thought of her denying me the curtesy of providing for her. She's mine to care for.

Maybe she needs a reminder of just how much I own every inch of her.

Gracie

As Vinny and Massio go to his office, I clutch Bonnie tighter against my chest, giving her a hug. "You're such a clever girl." She squeezes my cheeks and brings her lips to mine, delivering me a sloppy kiss and making me giggle. "You walked for Papa?"

"Papa!" she shouts, clear as day, and my heart hammers, and tears fill my eyes.

"She does love Vincent, that's for sure, and I've never seen him so attached to a little one." Hazel smiles in our direction. "I made us some hot cocoa." She tilts her head toward the patio, and I smile. She reminds me of my mother, but an older, wiser version, one I wish I could keep.

"Thank you."

"Come"—she gestures—"I have a blanket laid outside for Bonnie too, and there're some toys the grandchildren have left." As we step outside, she motions toward the plastic toy box, and I place Bonnie down on the blanket while she turns the outdoor heater up.

I take a seat on the huge sofa, with fluffy blankets and cushions, luxuries I've only ever witnessed on television. When I first arrived here for the Halloween party, I couldn't understand how this was someone's home, and a family member's at that. My father never spoke a good word about Vinny or his relatives, and even at a young age, I heard the jealousy in his tone.

"How's your day been?" Hazel asks, and I wrinkle my nose.

She lets out an almighty chuckle that makes her chest bounce and causes Bonnie to jolt. "That good?"

"I don't like malls."

Her eyebrows shoot up. "Well, that's different. So, what do you like? What did you do for fun at home?"

My mind wanders when I consider her question. "When I lived with my mother, it was on a ranch." Hazel nods along to my words, and excitement builds inside me as I tell her about my childhood. "We had stables and horses. Mine was Minnie, she had the glossiest brown coat and most brooding eyes. I'd ride her bareback until the sun went down. Even on the hottest of days, she'd ride for miles." I smile at the memory.

"Are the horses still at your mama's ranch?"

I shake my head. "I'm not sure. My father assured me he was caring for them, though." I play with the hem of my T-shirt, and she eyes me skeptically.

Then she clears her throat. "What else did you like, honey?"

"The church. I'm not religious, not like my mama anyway, but I like helping people."

She sits forward. "I go to church, and we have fundraisers, is that something you'd like to help with?"

I bite into my lip, looking at my lap, unwilling to commit to anything. "I'd have to ask Vinny."

She smiles and pats my leg. "You leave Vinny to me."

When I meet her eyes, I mirror the smile on her face. Something tells me Hazel is trying to get me to stay, and as tempting as it is, I want to go home.

Chapter Twenty-Four

Vinny

The room is blanketed in darkness when I slip inside.

After Massio left, I spent the next hour on the phone listening in on Rafael's breakdown of what he'd discovered during his torture of dealers. It was no shock to hear that Harrison Davis did indeed plant him inside the club, but our security intercepted him before the police arrived. The man certainly has a boner for our family, and as a thorn in our side, we will spend every waking day on edge until that damn thorn is removed.

Her soft snoozes are like a cloak of contentment whispering over my skin with each breath she takes, and as I stroke the tie with the tips of my fingers, I can't help but reevaluate my previous plans. Should I just let her sleep?

Pre-cum slides down the tip of my cock at imagining taking her in her sleep, so I watch the shadow of her small form while I undress. Was there really any other option?

Grabbing the tie, I make my way toward the top of the bed to stare down at her. Beautiful, every inch of her. Bringing a lock of her hair to my nostrils, I breathe her in, then let the silkiness slip from my fingertips and onto the pillow. I flick on the bedside light, and she stirs in her sleep. She stretches like a cat, and her pouty lips move, but she doesn't open her eyes, still deep enough in her slumber to allow me to carry out my devious plan. With the hook on her collar between my fingers, I thread the tie through it and wrap the other end around the bedframe. After moving down the bed, I grip her ankles and flip her onto her stomach, and she jolts with a loud squeal.

My cock bursts pre-cum at the noise, and my tongue thickens when I imagine taking her roughly, but I choose to pacify her instead. "It's okay, Little Pet, Daddy's here."

She exhales and her shoulders sag.

"Lift up onto your knees so Daddy can lick you."

With her elbows digging into the mattress, she pushes herself up onto her knees, leaving her ass and pussy exposed for me. "Good girl," I praise from behind her, stroking her toned asscheek. Without warning, I raise my palm and slap her ass hard, the crack reverberating through the room, and she releases a whimper that has my cock jumping with triumph. "That's a good little pet, taking Daddy's punishment."

Slap.

"Next time I tell you to do something"—*slap*—"you do it!" The sound of my palm connecting with her ass again has my cock leaking.

Slap.

"Apologize."

DOMINATION

She buries her head in the sheets, a sob emanating from her, and my heart seizes for a split second, then my blood rushes as her slickness gathers between her legs. "Such a greedy little slut for Daddy." My hand crashes against her asscheek.

"I-I'm sorry, Daddy." I yank the free end of the tie, using it as a rein to force her head where I want it to be.

Slap.

"I-I'm sorry."

Slap.

"I'll be a good girl." She sniffles. "I promise."

Gently, I stroke over her reddened ass, reveling in the way she pushes back against my hand. "Daddy's going to fill your cunt with his cum."

"Please ..."

"I'm going to force my baby inside you, Gracie."

Stepping forward, I push my cock into her tight opening, ramming into her small pussy hole. I groan as my cock sinks in and out of her, smearing her pussy juices and my pre-cum with every slide. My pelvis slams against her ass, and I piston into her, using her hole punishingly. I yank harder on the tie, wrapping it around my fist. "Fuck yes."

She moans, and my balls ache to release. "You like that, Little Pet? You like Daddy fucking you like a slut?"

Her pussy contracts around me, letting me know just how much she likes it. "Yes!" Her pussy muscles suck me in, the bed hits the wall with each rhythmic stroke, and her spine arches as her orgasm hits her.

"Jesus," I croak, pleasure zipping up my spine, and when my slit releases cum into her womb, I slam myself deeper, willing my seed to take form. "Give Daddy a baby, Little Pet," I mumble into her back as I fold over her. "Breed for Daddy," I pant out into the room, meaning every word, and we fall to the mattress in a sticky heap.

Gracie

Our heavy breaths fill the air, and I think he's going to lie beside me, but instead, he pulls back, taking me with him.

"I'm going to slide out of your little cunt, Gracie." My name on his tongue warms me, telling me I'm not another one of his little pets. I'm his Gracie. "Hold my cum in your pussy, Gracie. I'm going to instruct you on when to release it." Is that even possible? "I want to watch your pussy drip with my seed, then I'm going to push it back inside your tight little hole," he growls.

Oh, god, this man and his filthy mouth. I never in my wildest dreams realized any of what Vinny has opened me up to existed. A whimper leaves me when I imagine a life without it. He tugs on the tie, straightening my neck, the collar pulling me in line under his control.

Then his cock slips from me, and droplets of his warmth trickle down the inside of my thighs as I try to clench my pussy and hold it all in. His hot breath rasps over my ass, sending a flurry of goose bumps in its wake.

"Let it out, Gracie." He opens my asscheeks wide,

encouraging me to open up to him, then I push out, relaxing my pussy. "Fuck, that's beautiful, your little hole is dripping so epically." His tone is laced in wonderment as his thick finger scoops up the cum and prods at my opening, then he adds another finger. "Mm, Daddy would like to fist this tight little cunt."

Oh, sweet Jesus, what the hell? A fist? A high-pitched squeak leaves me, and he chuckles. "Not tonight, baby, I need to get my little pet ready for that." He's back to the little pet again, and my shoulders sag.

He must sense the change in me because he replaces his fingers with the tip of his cock and fists himself at my entrance before guiding the slick head of his cock to my asshole. My body pulls tight. "Shhh, Little Pet. Daddy wants to break all your holes in."

He starts by fisting himself at my back hole while his finger circles my clit. My body somehow relaxes, the forbidden sensation of feeling him back there has me melting into him.

He leans forward and delivers spittle into the cruck of my ass, then rubs the head of his cock up and down, blending the spittle with his cum.

Slowly, he pushes the tip against my asshole, and his hands find my hips, holding me in place, his fingertips so rough they're bruising.

"Oh," I pant, his thick tip stretching me further.

Inch by languorous inch, he pushes into me, the rhythm of his finger never slowing as his breathing becomes heavier against my back.

"That's it, such a good girl, letting Daddy take you

here," he coos into my neck, placing tender kisses down to my shoulders.

The head of his cock sinks inside me, past my muscled barrier, and I scream at the pain lancing through me.

"Oh fuck, Gracie. Feels so good."

I melt at his words, gripping onto the bed sheets to anchor me.

The fiery sensation in my ass becomes like molten lava, boiling to the surface from his savagery. "Shh, it's okay," he repeats, and pushes further inside.

I shake my head frantically. "I don't think I can do it," I whine.

His heavy pants fill the air, and his fingers twitch on my hips. "I'm nearly in, Gracie. Fuck. I'm nearly in," he rasps.

He moves a hand to press a finger on my clit, and I buck beneath him, the sensation sends a wave of arousal through me, and he slams inside me, stealing the air from my lungs. He wrenches on the tie, bringing my face to his, and I fall back against his chest, then he crashes his mouth over mine as I scream out the pain coupled with pleasure.

Thrust after thrust, I become his little pet.

His lips wrap around my nipple, caressing it, and he suckles. First, it's hungrily, his tongue flicking over the bud as he attempts to swallow my breast into his mouth like a frantic, unfed animal who can't get enough of me and my flavor. Then he slows to a steady pace that allows me to relax at his calmness. Both his actions are overwhelming, the crazed, possessiveness and the controlled look of splendor as he feeds from me.

Toying with his hair, I love the bristliness of his silver strands between my fingers, his maturity an aphrodisiac for me.

"Do you like me feeding from you?" he rasps, his slickness coating my leg.

"You know I do." He smiles against my breast, then pops off my nipple and lays his head back on the sheets, staring up at me.

"I'm taking you shopping tomorrow," he states, and I blink. Why on earth would he …

"You didn't buy anything for yourself, and you know damn well I expected you to." He raises an eyebrow, expecting me to argue.

"I can go by myself if you're busy."

"Absolutely. Fucking. Not. It killed me knowing you were out without me today."

I giggle, but his face is deadly serious. *Oh my.*

His gaze is transfixed on me as he flicks his tongue over my nipple, and milk bubbles to the surface. I expect him to suck on me, but he laps at it, allowing me to see the milk being drawn onto his tongue. Jeez, that's hot. I squirm and his lip curls. "We're having dinner with our family tomorrow."

Our family?

A coldness takes over me.

"The boys and their wives," he tacks on.

"We are?"

"Yes, Gracie, we are." His tone leaves no room for argument, so I don't even attempt it.

"Why did you stiffen earlier when I called you Little Pet?"

My eyes widen, and my mouth falls open. How did he pick up on that?

A chuckle vibrates his chest. "I'm a Mafia don, I take notice of every movement." Did I just voice my thoughts aloud? I give my head a shake.

"I don't know what you mean." The lie almost gets stuck in my throat, and I lift my chin slightly.

His eyes narrow, and his pupils darken with intent, then he shifts, raising up to his elbow to glare down at me. He looms over me, causing my breath to hitch, and wraps his hand around my throat and presses. "Don't lie to me, Little Pet. Tell me." Of course he saw right through me. Like he said, he's been trained to. I need to be more careful and to continue with my plan, the one I've come to hate.

"It made me feel disposable." Tears spring to my eyes, but I won't allow them to fall. His eyebrows furrow, and he tilts my head to the side to access my jawline, where he peppers soft kisses down my face and over my neck, licking around my collar. "I could never replace you, Gracie. Nor do I ever want to." My heart lurches in my chest, and a squeezing sensation causes my lungs to struggle to function. Yet he appears completely unaware and continues kissing down my body, bringing with it pleasure and pain blending into one. I finally allow the tears to fall, but I disguise the pain his words cause and throw my head back in passion.

Chapter Twenty-Five

Vinny

As the morning sun broke into the bedroom, I took delight in the fact that Gracie opened up to me last night, even after taking her ass so abruptly.

She lay on my chest all night, with my arm wrapped around her, and I dropped tender kisses on her head between whispering sweet gestures in her ear.

The idea of her growing up in anything other than a loving home makes me furious, and at hearing her restless sleep, I wonder what other secrets she hides.

Does she dream about the needles in her sleep? Is that what keeps her awake at night? I need to speak with Rafael and make him aware that I have no intention of letting her father live, not after discovering how poorly he treated his daughter. I'll be damned if he ever gets the opportunity to be near either of my girls again. It's not worth finishing with his treatment in rehab. It's costing us a fortune, and ultimately, he's going to die. Maybe I should just put the sorry sack of shit out of his misery now.

Thoughts of Nancy flash in the forefront of my mind, annoying the fuck out of me. I mean, I tried my best for her son, but I know the woman who raised him would not want her granddaughter and great-granddaughter to suffer in the way Gracie has and still does. Nope, I owe her that much; Robert is a lost cause, and it's high time I accepted it.

"Gracie?"

She stirs groggily, and I smile at the way she lifts her head and stretches like a little cat. "Hmm?"

"I'm taking you to breakfast. No serving me under the table today," I quip.

Her head rises, and she attempts to flatten her tousled hair. "You are?"

"Yes, baby, I am."

Her bright-blue eyes flash with delight, and I love it. I want to see that look every damn day for the rest of my life. I rub over the pain in my chest, my heart hammering precariously fast at the thought of us having forever.

"I need you to be ready in half an hour. Can you do that for me?"

"Uh-huh." She nods like she is dumbstruck.

"Good girl." I throw the sheet off us both, then rise from the bed. "Up." Bending over, I slap her ass, then wince when I remember the lack of aftercare last night. It's almost as if I've given up on the submissiveness of a pet, and instead, it's formed into a relationship of acceptance. One I like maybe a little too much.

Still, aftercare is just as important for a partner, so

with that thought in mind, I stride toward the bathroom to grab the soothing lotion from the cabinet.

When I return, my entire body stills, my breath stolen from my lungs. Jesus, she's stunning, beautiful and innocence combined.

Purity at its rarest.

"Vinny, you're staring at me." She tilts her head and lets out a small giggle.

My heart kicks a beat at the way she uses my name, and I delight in the feelings she brings out of me. Flicking the cap on the lotion, I make my way over to her. "Daddy needs to take care of you," I soothe, grazing my fingers over her reddened ass cheeks. "Then we're going to shower, and I'm going to fill you with cum again before we leave for breakfast."

She glances over her shoulder, her eyebrows furrowing. "Fill me again?

"Hmm," I croon. "I can't get enough of you."

Color rises from her chest and up her face, and I don't miss the excitement in her eyes. Fuck, I want to give her that joy every goddamn day of her life.

"Now, open your legs for me to take care of you."

Gracie

After Vinny and I showered, he filled me with cum and brought me to orgasm. He told me it's the first time he's been late in his life and he didn't like it, but he was smiling, leaving me uncertain as to how much he didn't like it.

He took Bonnie from her crib to allow me time to get dressed and left me with strict instructions not to shower again but to wear panties.

My ass is sore and the wetness between my legs coats the inside of my thighs with each step, and when I hear his deep chuckle from the kitchen as he speaks to Bonnie, more of his cum slips from me, causing the fabric to become wetter.

There's nothing hotter than a strong man playing with a baby, and when I lean my hip against the doorframe, I'm conflicted. Bonnie hasn't had a male role model before now, but neither have I. Is it cruel of me to take her away from the man she clearly adores?

She's in the new highchair that Hazel ordered for her,

and Vinny is sitting opposite her, scooping up the freshly prepared food suitable for a baby.

"Here we are, Bon-Bon, another spoonful of yummy." Vinny swoops the spoon down into Bonnie's waiting mouth, and she happily accepts it. "Clever girl." My stomach twists with hope, and an incredible sense of guilt too. I'm stealing this from her, from them both.

Massio clears his throat, and when Vinny lifts his head, he jerks his chin in my direction, making Vinny aware of my presence.

My spine bolts straight, and I scan Massio, wondering if he will be joining us on our outing today. Who am I kidding? Of course he will. Vinny is a Mafia don; wherever he is, there's danger. Echoing my thoughts, Massio checks the clip on his gun, then tucks it into his waistband. My eyes flick over to Vinny, who is watching me with narrowed eyes, and a gun tucked behind his back has reality hitting me like a Mack truck.

I need to continue with my plan if I want my daughter to have the life she deserves.

"Pa!" Bonnie shrieks with glee, and Vinny's face breaks out into an amazing smile, and he turns his attention back toward her. Her words and his actions have my insides twisting and my legs feeling like they're going to buckle.

What the hell am I doing?

"Papa is going shopping with momma." He turns to face me, pulling me from my wayward thoughts. "Because momma was a bad girl and couldn't do as she was told yesterday." I roll my eyes, and his upper lip twitches. "Come say your goodbyes." He holds his hand out to haul me toward him, then he places a kiss on top of my head and strokes my hair like he's unable to help himself. "Then meet us outside, Massio and I need to discuss business." I nod like an obedient pet.

My eyes catch onto Massio, and I swear he's wearing a glare of contempt, but it's quickly masked, and only when they leave the room do I breathe a sigh of relief.

"Morning, my little Bon-Bon," I coo, stealing Vinny's nickname for her, and as soon as the words leave my lips, the familiar sliver of guilt trickles into my veins and nausea courses through me, causing me to clutch the kitchen counter.

"Are you okay, honey?" Hazel's concerned voice filters through my senses, and I nod, but she doesn't seem convinced. "Should I tell Vinny you're not feeling well?"

I stand taller, releasing the counter. "I'm fine."

She tilts her head, eyeing me skeptically. "If you say so."

Can she see right through the lies? The betrayal? Does she see what's right in front of her?

Can Massio see it too?

Chapter Twenty-Six

Vinny

I take a puff of my cigar while Massio gives me a brief rundown of what I will be missing today. Not that I care. Since Gracie and Bonnie entered my life, I feel more and more like Mafia life is slipping away from me.

"Are you even listening?" Massio clips. "Jesus, Vinny, she has your head screwed up." He whirls his finger around at the side of his head, implying I'm going crazy. He's not wrong. I've never been so obsessed over a woman. He crosses his arms over his chest and broadens his feet. "She's hiding something."

"Hmm," I muse, dragging my finger over my lip, a habit of mine even I find annoying.

His eyebrows shoot up. "You know?"

"She's the woman from the Halloween party," I say out loud for the first time.

He rears back, stunned. "And she knows you know?"

I lean back in my chair. "Of course."

"And she's your pet?" He winces, choking the words out. Massio has always been uncomfortable around my pets; he never knows where to look or how to act around them.

"Sort of." I drag a hand through my hair.

"Sort of?" He shakes his head. "You treat her different to the others, Vinny."

"I do," I admit. "She's my granddaughter." A smirk plays on my lips, and I shrug my shoulder.

Massio blanches. "Jesus. You're fucked up."

"I know." I grin and my cock hardens. "She's hiding things from me. But my little pet is delicate, she's slowly opening, and I don't want to scare her. She has a troubled past."

His spine bolts upright, and his glare turns deadly. If there's one thing neither of us can stand, it's abusers. "Any ideas what she's hiding?"

"She has nightmares. Robert was abusing her." I don't elaborate further, what Gracie told me is ours. He doesn't need to know the true depths of her terror.

"You want him dead?"

I cluck my tongue. "He's in rehab. Rafael arranged the placement; I'd like you to work with him and have him moved to the warehouse when it's convenient."

Retribution flashes in his eyes, and he knows exactly why I want him at the warehouse; it's the end of the line for Robert. "You got it, sir." This is what I like about Massio, he's loyal to the bone.

Stubbing out the cigar, I give him a swift nod; he pushes back in his chair and pulls open the door, revealing Hazel. She has her hand raised like she was about to knock. Massio steps aside to allow her entry.

Instantly, my body is on high alert. "Hazel?"

Her hand wafts through the air, mimicking swatting a fly, and she chuckles. "She's fine, relax. I just want to speak to you about her." She wrings her hand in front of her, and I motion for her to take the seat Massio vacated.

When the door clicks shut, I turn my attention to her. "Go on."

"She's lonely, Vinny."

I grind my teeth but ignore her. She shouldn't be lonely, not when she has me.

"The poor girl doesn't see anyone besides me and you." She blows out a deep breath.

"She doesn't talk of any friends, it's almost like she's been isolated. She dreams of being at her mother's home, on the ranch?"

I nod.

"She had horses there, and she seems to think her father is caring for them?" Her eyes are full of hope. Hope I'm about to crumble.

I shake my head, and her shoulders sag. "He sold the horses a couple of years ago. He offered some to me. If I'd known ..." I leave my words open, and she tilts her head.

Then she straightens her shoulders. "I've been thinking, maybe she could join my local church." A cruel laugh erupts from me, and Hazel's eyes narrow. A fucking church?

"Vincent Marino, don't be so rude." Her stern, hurt voice drains the humor from me.

Hazel has been good to my family over the years, and

with the way she scowls at me now, I know I've hurt her. I clear my throat. "My apologies."

She lifts her chin. "We have a church group that runs tomorrow evening. There's only a dozen of us, and you know I'd look after her, we organize food parcels for the underprivileged."

I strum my fingers on the desk while I contemplate it.

"We do charitable work, Vinny, nothing nefarious."

I balk at her comment. "And what is it you expect me to get out of this?" I snipe.

She rolls her lip, then meets my eyes. "Maybe if you showed her she wasn't just another one of your pets, she might like to stay around longer." She glares at me, and I narrow my eyes. Her words are like a warning going off in my head, and my pulse rushes, causing my temple to pulsate.

I lean forward in my seat, my body on high alert. The thought of her planning to leave me has my blood pumping furiously. "Has she said something?"

"No. Only that she misses home. She talks about it a lot."

I scoff; there's no way in hell she's missing that prick.

"Her real home, the one where she grew up with her mother," Hazel states, in such a way, I question if she's hearing my thoughts.

"I'll think about it."

Her eyes gleam with triumph, and I roll mine. "I said I'd think about it, Hazel," I bite out, hoping she understands.

With the excitement in her eyes, and the way she

jumps up, I know she doesn't. Fantastic, I'm about to destroy an old woman's spirit.

"You're a good man, Vincent." She pats my hand, and I open my mouth to clarify my words, but she's out the door before I can utter a single one.

"Fuck," I groan, dragging a hand through my hair, knowing I need to use Massio's second-in-command, Felix, to escort them to fucking church.

The horn to my SUV beeps, and I glance at my watch. Yeah, Massio is ready to leave, because the fucker wants to get back for the game this afternoon.

Pushing back on my chair, I head toward the door and into the day ahead. A day of spoiling my little pet.

Another new experience for me.

With my feet crossed at the ankles, I lean back against the blacked-out SUV and wait for her. The moment she comes into view, every nerve on my body comes alive with a silly flutter I thought was reserved solely for young love.

She smiles in my direction, and our eyes remain locked with each step she takes, but her footing wavers when she glances toward Massio. My body locks up tight, and I drop my feet to the floor as envy rushes through my veins like a rampant drug, stealing the joy from within me and replacing it with venom.

My jaw clenches, and her eyes narrow in on the action. Then I throw open the SUV door and hold out my hand for her to climb inside, ignoring the way her eyes flick over my face with concern. Tucking her safely into her seat, I pull the seatbelt over her slender waist, straightening it at her shoulder and clicking it in place.

"Th-thank you." Her innocent voice breezes over me, washing away the anger from only moments ago.

I let out a breath and stroke her hair with the tenderness I reserve solely for her.

When I step back and shut the door, Massio is watching me with knitted brows. "You're so fucked." He grins, earning him the middle finger as I round the vehicle.

Slipping in beside her, I waste no time moving the hair from her face and tucking it behind her ear, then I lean further in. "I don't like your attention on other men, Little Pet." She flinches and stiffens, then opens her mouth to speak, but I shake my head, and she snaps her mouth shut. "You don't look at them unless it's to speak to them, do you hear me?" I toy with her collar before tugging on it, reminding her of who her owner is.

She nods.

"Use your words," I coax, and press kisses down the column of her neck. Unable to help myself, my tongue traces over her flesh. Fuck, I'd love to mark it with something more permanent that tells everyone she's mine.

"Y-yes, Daddy." She chews on her bottom lip.

"Now, open your legs nice and wide and push your panties to the side. I want your slick cunt on display, dripping with my cum while you suck on me." Triumph flares in my chest at the way her eyes bulge and her mouth falls open. I lean back and unbuckle my belt, lower my zipper, then pull out my throbbing cock. "You're going to suck

DOMINATION

Daddy all the way to the restaurant, and if you're a good girl later, I'll let you swallow my cum." Her cheeks redden, and I relish it. Glancing up, I catch Massio staring back at me. *Yes, fuckwit, I control and own every inch of her.* Then she sinks her mouth down on my cock, and my lips part while I hold his stare. She slides her panties to the side, tucking them in her asscheek, and I delight in knowing my cum has marked her.

My fingers tangle in her silky locks. "Daddy's little pet is a slut for cock, isn't that right, Gracie?"

She attempts to lift her head, but I hold it in place, taking great delight in the way Massio flicks his eyes away.

"Good girl," I croon, resting my free arm over the back of the seat.

Mine.

Chapter Twenty-Seven

Vinny

Massio steps forward and takes hold of my elbow when I step out of the SUV. "Was that really necessary?" he hisses in my ear, and I glare down to his grasp before slicing my gaze up toward his.

He pales and swallows thickly, dropping his hand in the process. "I'm not interested in your girl, Vinny." His eye implore mine.

"I know that. Just making sure she knows who owns her." I smirk and breeze past him to round the vehicle to unclip her.

The blush that creeps over her face as she steps out is adorable, and the way she lowers her eyes when her hand slips into mine is simply perfect. "Good girl," I whisper next to her ear, and she shudders.

Stepping inside the restaurant, I march toward the private room reserved solely for us and throw a venomous glare in the server's direction when he attempts to pull out Gracie's chair. Taking it from him, I hold it out for her, then she slips onto the seat, and I slide her beneath the table.

When the server hands us the menus, I watch in fascination as Gracie scans over it; her eyes bounce all over the page, and heat creeps up over her neck. She looks on the verge of a panic attack.

"What's wrong?"

She rolls her lip into her mouth but doesn't lift her face to answer me. It's almost like she's shutting down. Does she have an eating disorder? Hazel mentioned she barely eats.

For the first time since meeting her, I look at her in a new light. She's petite, slim build, almost fragile. My teeth ache, and I realize I'm clenching them.

She clears her throat. "May I have some fruit please?"

Her soft voice is clouded with uncertainty, but I decide to test the boundaries. "What about pancakes with the fruit?"

"They do pancakes?"

I glance down at the menu, suddenly unsure. They will create anything I order; I do, after all, own the damn place. Sure enough, there are pancakes.

"Page two, bottom of the page."

She flips the page over and squints, then quickly places the menu down. "Can I have buttermilk ones please?"

"Do you want chocolate chips?"

She nods coyly, with her hair acting as a curtain to hide her features, but my focus remains on her. She's skittish, a nervousness about her I haven't witnessed before.

DOMINATION

Alarm bells ring in my head, telling me something is off, but what, I'm unsure.

"What fruit would you like?"

She blinks, then clears her throat. "Apple?"

My eyes ping-pong over her face. "Apple?"

She nods.

Just a fucking apple?

"Look at the menu and tell me what else you'd would like." I gesture toward the menu, but she doesn't make a move to look at it. She needs more than a fucking apple, and I'd like to get her diet right, given the fact she could be carrying my baby.

"Apple is good."

My temper flares; she's evading my instructions, and it pisses me off. "Gracie." A growl emits from me, and I lean forward with a menacing glare. "Look at the menu and tell me what other fruit you'd like."

Tears fill her eyes, and her bottom lip wobbles, but she does as I ask and picks up the menu. "Orange, please." The way she says please so delicately and full of uncertainty has a need to comfort her coursing through me. My hands have balled into fists, and I exhale, knowing I'm about to trip her up like the bastard I am. Something tells me there's more to this.

"Anything else?" There's an abundance of other exotic and rare fruits available, and I'm sure she'd love to try them.

Her lips part. "No."

"No?" I crook an eyebrow.

The server arrives back at the table, and I watch her with fascination, relieved that she doesn't give the server any more attention than necessary, but she appears very uncomfortable as she fidgets from side to side.

Knowing she needs reassurance, I lean over the table and entwine our hands. "Tell him exactly what you'd like, and he'll bring it." I lock eyes with hers, hoping she can sense the truth behind my words. "Anything," I breathe out. Any-damn-thing. More than a fucking apple with a few pancakes.

She shuffles in her chair and straightens her shoulders. "May I order buttermilk pancakes and an apple please?"

"Yes, Miss." He nods, then turns toward me. "Sir?"

"Bring her a platter of every fruit you have. I'll have pastries and coffee. Gracie, orange juice?"

"Yes please," she squeaks.

When the server leaves, she glances around the empty room.

"It's my private room. This is my restaurant."

Her eyes light up, and a slow smile spreads over her pretty face. My chest puffs out with pride, knowing I put that smile there. "It's very nice."

My lip twitches. "Come sit on my lap." I push the chair back and make room for her. She steps around the table, and as soon as she's within reach, I tug her onto my lap and band an arm around her to hold her in place. "That's better." I nuzzle into her hair and kiss her neck just below her collar, and her body relaxes against me, almost like we've become one.

"I'm worried you have an eating disorder," I state, and she tenses. "Shh, it's okay." I deliver my words with kisses of reassurance while stroking her back up and down. "I know you're keeping something from me, Gracie." She freezes, and I hate it because she just gave herself away, and I also hate the fact she doesn't trust me enough to tell me her secrets.

"I don't have an eating disorder," she shoots back.

"You can tell me anything, you know that, right?"

"I trust you," she says, playing with the hair at the nape of my neck.

This earns her a deep ironic chuckle. "I'm a criminal, Gracie." Her body becomes taut, and I wish I could take the words back, but ultimately, she needs to hear them. "I'm not a good man."

"You're good to me. You're a good man to Bonnie, and you're good to your family." I love the fact she's fighting for my honor against even me.

I shake my head solemnly. "I haven't been a good father to my sons, Gracie," I admit, hating the way it stings my tongue on the way out. Her breathing becomes rapid, and I can sense her wanting to slip off my lap, so I tighten my hold on her. "And the worst part is, I wouldn't change that." A shallow whimper escapes her, and she blinks away the tears threatening to spill from her bright-blue eyes. I hate the emotion stuck there, like it's trapped. Like my words have instilled some horror inside her. But I need her to know what I am. What I truly am.

"I trust you," she repeats, almost brokenly, as though convincing herself.

"Maybe you shouldn't, Little Pet." I nuzzle into her stiff form. "Maybe you signed your life away to be caged for eternity with a savage."

"Maybe eternity is my cage, and the savage is my life."

My heart skips a beat at the thought of her choosing to be with me. Be damned with my age, the Mafia life, and the obstacles that might arise from all of it. "You don't mean that, little one." I press delicate kisses to her neck and over her shoulder.

"Yes, I do, Daddy."

Gracie

He knows I have a secret.

"Maybe you shouldn't, Little Pet." His kisses stoke the embers of the flames threatening to burn me from the inside out. "Maybe you signed your life away to be caged in eternity with a savage."

Maybe it's my destiny to be in a cage. Like a bird with clipped wings. Always yearning to see the beauty and freedom that lies beyond the steel bars. I've come to accept the fact I'll never know what it feels like to stretch my wings because they'll never have a chance to grow.

"Maybe eternity is my cage, and the savage is my life," I reply cooly, feeling anything but inside.

Did I just admit I want to stay with him? "You don't mean that, little one." I sway against him as his kisses send a flurry of excitement over me.

"Yes, I do, Daddy." With my face resting on his chest, I feel his heart skip a beat, and I revel in the fact I'm having the same effect on him as he has on me.

"You spoil me with your innocence, Little Pet." His

thick hand rocks me back and forth over his lap, and his length thickens against my leg, causing me to clench my thighs together.

The server breaks the silence when he places down the food and drinks, not making eye contact with Vinny or me. Vinny leans over and pulls a plate toward me, then selects a multitude of fresh fruits to place on the plate.

"Open," he grunts, bringing a strawberry to my mouth. I do as he asks. "That's a good girl," he praises.

One after the other, he selects items, then wipes the corner of my mouth with the napkin, causing butterflies to swirl in my stomach. "Would you like a drink?"

"Yes, please."

His cock jumps when I speak, and I bite into my lip to stifle the moan building in my chest.

He reaches for the orange juice and pours me a fresh glass, then brings the glass to my lips and holds the back of my head while guiding me toward the glass. "Good girl for taking your juice."

My pussy clenches at the way he cares for me, and when his hand strokes over my hair and down my spine, tingling follows in its wake.

He shifts in his chair, then, with his free hand, he strokes over the hard length of his cock. "I haven't given you your vitamins today," he mumbles on a low chuckle.

I lean forward and place a kiss on his throat, and he hisses through his teeth. "I want it." I breathe him in before pulling back, and when he turns his head to face me, his pupils are blown and desire mars his features. He looks two seconds away from exploding. Two seconds away from throwing me on the table and fucking me with the savage power I know he possesses. Slickness coats my thighs with each heavy breath he takes. "You're a little slut for Daddy, aren't you?"

Arousal clouds my vision, and I sway in his arms, the headiness of our interaction taking its toll on me. He commands every part of me, and I welcome it. "Yes," I pant.

"Hmm, I bet you'd do whatever I asked of you, wouldn't you, Little Pet?"

"Yes, Daddy."

His eyes blaze with fire, and his nostrils flare. "Pre-cum is leaking from the tip of my cock, and I want nothing more than to spill it over these delectable lips." He uses his thumb to roughly swipe over my bottom lip. "Cover your pretty little face in my warm cum and leave it there so everyone can see who marked you." He strokes up my cheek and then back down, all the way to my neck where he wraps his hand around my throat. His fingers twitch against me. "I'd force my thick cock so deep inside your throat you wouldn't be able to breathe. Tell me, Little Pet, would you like that too?"

Why the hell do I like the sound of that so much? His roughness as well as his tenderness.

All I can do is nod. All other coherent thoughts are banished, like I'm under his command.

He chuckles, breaking the spell of consumption. Then his fingers flex against my delicate skin, and he tilts me back. "Open your mouth, Little Pet."

My eyes ping-pong over his face, searching for his reasoning, but with his hand around my throat, I don't care why he wants me in this position. Truthfully, he can have me any way he craves. I open my mouth, and he leans over me, his solid, taut form filled with brutality as he lowers his face toward mine and ever so slowly delivers a stream of spittle into my mouth, over my lips, and finally, down my neck. His eyes glint with lust, and a hum of approval grunts from deep inside him.

Then without warning, he pulls me upright, coated in his spit. "You can swallow it, Gracie." He lifts me to my feet, and I sway with a lightheadedness from the shock of his actions while my clit throbs, eager for more. "Come. We have shopping to do." He taps my ass as he rises from his chair, leaving me astounded and confused. My body sways in the haze of lust he's placed me in.

How can he be so aroused one minute, then it's gone just as quick?

A deep chuckle reverberates from him, and I focus my gaze on his. When his thumb rubs over my cheek, I feel the wetness of his spittle being rubbed into my skin. "You look stunned, Little Pet. It's fucking adorable and such a turn-on seeing my spit on your chest." My hand moves toward it, but he pushes it away. "Leave it there, I like seeing it." His eyes blaze with an intoxicating intensity threatening every atom inside me. Then he dusts his lips lightly over my cheek followed by a seductive lick of his lips. "Don't worry, be a good girl, and Daddy will tend to that ache between your legs."

My eyes widen; how does he know?

"I can smell your arousal, Gracie." My body heats with fire, and I open my mouth to tell him he can't possibly, then I snap it shut with the look of amusement on his face. "Don't worry, Little Pet. I'm hungry too." He places my hand on his thick cock, and my breath stutters. "Fuck, you feel good," he groans, and squeezes my hand with his large one, and I can't help but to stroke the tip of his cock with my thumb, delighting in the way his muscles coil beneath my touch.

My daddy might control every inch of me, but I control him too.

Chapter Twenty-Eight

Vinny

After leaving the restaurant, my cock was as solid as a fucking rock. The buckle of my belt chaffed the tip, and it hurt like a bitch. Still, I was determined to make sure Gracie suffered just as much as me. I wasn't lying when I said I could smell her pussy. Her arousal calls to me, and fuck me, does she smell divine, especially with my cum dripping from her.

In the SUV, I clipped the seatbelt over her, and while driving to the mall, I caressed her clit over her wet panties, but never enough to bring her to full orgasm. No, she will do that with my cock nestled deep inside her, pumping her full of my seed with determination for it to take form.

Walking through the mall, I grip her hand in mine. This is a new concept to me, and I'm aware being out in public showing affection toward her is pinning a target on her back, but I'm confident in the security I have in place around me and my girl at all times to not care too much. What she doesn't know, is this means she will always be of high value to not just me but my enemies too, so while I have always been strategic in my display of affection, today, I couldn't give a fuck. Quite frankly, I've never cared about anyone enough to justify their protection, but now, I relish it. Her small hand in mine as we walk through the foyer has me drawing her fingers toward my lips, giving her open affection I've never shown anyone else.

Glancing at the gold sign of "Opaque" above the shop I want to take her, I take a deep breath and hope like hell one of my old submissives isn't working today.

Luck is not on my side.

The moment we enter the shop, this feels like a mistake. A grave fucking mistake. "Vinny!" she shrieks, setting my teeth on edge, and the way Gracie shrinks back beside me has my arm pulling her tightly against my chest. Her fingers wrap around my sleeve, holding me against her. It's like she's terrified to be in the store.

"Cindy. This is Gracie. I'd like you to take good care of her." My tone is stern and clear, the meaning behind the words unmistakable. *Don't fuck with her*.

Her jaw tightens as she takes Gracie in. Then something shines in Cindy's eyes, and she glances toward Gracie's collar before snapping her eyes back to mine, masking the cruel gleam in an instant.

"Bad idea, sir," Massio grunts in my ear, but I refuse to listen. She'll do as she's fucking told or reap the consequences.

DOMINATION

"My name is Selina. What is it she needs?" Her eyes bore into me with vengeance.

"Everything," I state, ignoring the fact I got her name slightly wrong.

"The usual, then?" Her smile taunts me, and not for the first time in my life, I could happily drain the life from a woman's eyes. Gracie drops her hold on me and steps to my side, almost out of reach, and I hate the movement. My teeth grind and I side-eye her.

She's acting nonchalant, looking at everything in the store but me and Cindy ... or Selina, who the fuck ever.

"She can have anything she wants."

Selina rolls her eyes, and in the past, that move would have had me spanking the brat out of her asscheeks, but today, all I see is a woman with a shitty attitude trying to belittle someone else while disrespecting me.

She eyes Gracie up and down, not even attempting to hide her contempt. Then with a cluck of her tongue she opens her mouth. "Follow me, and I'll make it work somehow." When she spins on her heels and heads toward the fitting rooms, I'm about to tell Gracie I'll be there in a minute, but she struts past me without a second glance and follows Selina.

"She's pissed at you," Massio states, like I don't know.

I drag a finger over my lip as she disappears into the fitting room. "I realize."

"You knew the girl worked here. You gave her the fucking job," he spits out with venom, shocking the hell out of me. I swallow back the lump gathered in my throat, and panic crawls up my spine. How the hell am I supposed to remember who works here on what days.

Guilt rears its ugly head. Gracie is delicate, the last thing I want is someone with a spiteful tongue knocking her confidence and hurting her.

"I wasn't thinking," I snap back, pissed at myself.

"Well, she's going to fucking love making Gracie feel like shit." He gestures toward the fitting room, causing my temple to pulsate. I don't like her being in there with her spilling her poison. "She's not like any of your other girls." His words are an understatement. Damn fucking right she's not like any of the other girls.

She's the only girl.

"I'll make her pay, don't you fucking worry," I grind out, striding toward the fitting room, and a belly laugh sounds from Massio.

Fucker.

Gracie

I can't believe he brought me here. He brought me to a store where one of his old submissives works. Great, just freaking great.

"You know, you're not his usual type." The dark-haired beauty with a hand on her hip scans my body with a raised eyebrow and a twist of her lips.

"Maybe he wanted something different," I tell her, trying and failing miserably to disguise the tremor in my voice. I hate feeling like this—inadequate. It's why I feel so comfortable in my community church, everyone is accepted. It doesn't matter what your background is or what you're capable of, everyone is welcome.

"You wouldn't be able to handle the real Vinny, his darkness and all." Her cruel taunt sends a shiver down my spine. "I don't think any of us truly would," she mumbles to herself so low I don't think I'm meant to hear it. I can handle anything Vinny gives me; I welcome it.

"Has he taken you to his basement, his dungeon, to play with you?" My face falls and my stomach rolls at the fact he hasn't done that, but I quickly school my features. "Amazing, isn't it?" she gloats. "All the incredible things he has down there," she continues while I try to suppress the whimper building inside. Why is he keeping things from me? Does he see me as fragile? Unable to handle him?

"Still"—her lip curls in distaste—"I don't know what he sees in you."

My heart freefalls when I think about him holding back to appease me. Is that what he does? Does he see me as a delicate toy who will break easily? Doesn't he realize how strong I truly am?

"Ah, bless." She toys with the collar Vinny made me. Then her lips pout into a ducklike pose. "He didn't even get you the real thing." She huffs and pushes off the doorframe to circle me, like a hunter rounding up its prey.

Her heels click with each movement, and the fitted black dress she wears has me darting my eyes away. She looks like a grown up compared to me in my flimsy, worn dress. No wonder Vinny brought me here. "You're young too." She flicks my hair with her finger. "Barely even have tits." That's a lie, my breasts are practically bulging against the fabric of my summer dress, full of milk. "And your stomach isn't even flat." There's a sneer on her lips as she glances down toward my stomach, but I'm struggling to make out the issue. I know I have a pouch since giving birth to Bonnie, but I wasn't aware it was a problem.

She turns and leaves the room while I exhale.

When she returns only moments later, she drops a

pile of clothes at my feet. "I wouldn't have thought a little girl like you would want someone like Vinny."

"I'm not a little girl," I snap. She's starting to piss me off.

Just what the hell was he thinking?

"You've been in his dungeon, so you know what he likes." She kicks at the red thong by her foot while wearing a spiteful smile.

Her words have a hint of curiosity to them; she's testing how much I know. The fact she knows something which I don't has my veins swirling with disappointment, but why should I feel any different from the others, maybe I am just like them.

"Aww," she mock pouts, and I want to tell her lips might get stuck like that, but I don't want to lower myself to her level. "He didn't, did he?"

She pats my shoulder in a patronizing gesture. "Don't worry. I don't think you'd be able to handle what goes on down there anyway."

Jealousy courses through me, and I hate it.

Instead of showing her how inadequate I feel, I act unperturbed, but inside, my heart constricts, and my legs tremble with a need to flee. Tears spring to my eyes, but I refuse to let them fall. I won't let a bully like her beat me. I've had what feels like a lifetime of them, and I won't take it any longer. My hands ball into fists as she continues ticking off a list of issues she has with me.

The door to the fitting room swings open, and as quick as it draws my attention, I move my gaze away from the man who caused me my distress in the first place. His eyes are attempting to bore into my soul and pull it out in the tattered form that it is, then mold it back together with his sweet words and gentle affection.

"Is everything okay?"

I choke on thin air. *Is he serious right now?*

"Yes, Daddy." I flinch at her words. Daddy? It's like a punch to my gut, and my heart skips a beat at the stark reminder he's had other women call him this.

I'm disposable.

I'm nothing more than another little pet, to be used and discarded, toyed with and forgotten.

Jealousy and self-loathing combine, surging from deep inside me, and heat rushes through my veins, baring my feelings to them both as my cheeks flame. I want to curl up in a ball, to run for the door, to cry and beat my fists against Vinny's strong chest.

I want him to want me.

Me.

The broken, unwanted, unloved girl who only feels whole when her daddy loves her back.

Vinny's jaw sharpens.

"Everything is fine. We're just choosing your new little pet's panties. Isn't that right, Grace?" she announces proudly with a flirtatious smile, making me jolt at her change in demeanor? I hate her. My eyes flare with anger toward Vinny as well as the catty woman who thinks she can degrade me.

Vinny steps into the room and closes the door behind him, and I take a step back, not missing the way his nostrils flare.

His jaw clenches, and his palms twitch as he balls his fists and uncurls them, only to repeat the process. I feel

DOMINATION

the heat emitting from him, and as much as I want to throw myself at him, I'm too hurt to move.

"Show me what you chose." He gestures toward the clothes on the floor, and a smug smile spreads over her face. Something tells me she'd take anything Vinny gives her and twist it into praise.

She slowly digs round the clothes, then lifts a pair of the lacy red panties on the tip of her finger. "I remember how much you liked red lace, Daddy." She beams, and my heart thumps wildly against my chest.

Vinny's venomous sneer toward her causes my pulse to race. His nostrils flare, his eyes darken, then he masks the anger and replaces it with a patronizing smile, one just as sinister as his cruel glare. He drags a calculating finger over his lips. "I didn't say you could call me daddy. Gracie is my little pet, isn't that right, Gracie?"

The woman's smile falls from her pretty face, and as much as I want to smile back at her, I'm too angry to delight in her disappointment.

Vinny's eyes drill into mine, the intensity radiating from him consumes me, and my pulse kicks up when I realize he's waiting on a response. He inches toward me as though he's unsure. When he reaches me, he tucks my hair behind my ears. "Trust me?" he whispers against my ear and places a tender kiss on my cheek. Then he turns my head and lowers his lips to mine before pulling back and eyeing me skeptically.

"Y-yes."

"Good girl, Little Pet. Good girl, my Gracie," he croons, in a velvety tone that has my anger fluttering away like it was never there. My Gracie?

He backs away and stands taller, then clears his throat. "Take off your dress, Gracie."

My heart rate kicks up, and my eyes meet his in the full-length mirror. He gives me a stern nod, and I swallow hard, knowing damn well that woman is still in the room watching me.

My fingers tremble as I step out of my tennis shoes and kick them to the side. I can feel their eyes on me, but I ignore them and lift my dress over my head, and when I make out the bulge in Vinny's pants, it gives me the confidence I need to do as he asks. Dropping my dress to the floor, I love the way Vinny sucks on his teeth and shoves his hands into his pant pockets like he's struggling to not touch me. I shake my head, knowing how much he loves my blonde locks and the silky feel of them. My hair brushes over the top of my ass, and he shifts from foot to foot. Then I glance over my shoulder and deliver the words I know he craves. "What now, Daddy?"

His Adam's apple slides slowly down his throat. "Hands on the mirror."

I lean forward and place my hands on the mirror.

"M-maybe I should leave." The woman moves, inching toward the exit.

"Stay the fuck where you are," Vinny fires out in a deadly tone he's never used with me, and my lip twitches at the way she freezes and her face pales. Her eyes are wide like a deer caught in headlights.

Vinny's fingers work through my hair, and I preen at the way the tips massage my scalp, then he yanks hard, straightening my neck, and our gazes lock in the mirror. He whispers, "You like that, Gracie? You like when I put the bitch in her place?" and his breath sends a shiver racing down my spine.

"Look at her panties," he demands, and Selina slices her gaze over to my panties. "Her little cotton panties that drive Daddy wild. I want to slide them to the side and thrust up inside her tiny cunt until she screams for me to stop. Isn't that right, Little Pet?"

"Yes, Daddy."

"I don't want red lace. Red lace was for the whores I fucked. This little pet is for keeps."

My heart swells on his words, and Selina's eyes widen, and her mouth falls open. The look of shock on her face makes my chest swell with confidence.

I swallow hard and nuzzle his cheek, and he sucks in a sharp breath. "Tell Cindy here what Daddy likes to do to you." He didn't call her by her name, and I revel in it. Then he rests his palm on my stomach. "Tell her what I'm going to give you."

My breathing becomes labored and my footing wavers, but his firm grip on my hip holds me steady.

Then he whispers, "Tell her I'm putting my baby in you." My heart skips a beat, and when he pulls back, my shoulders sag, but the sound of him frantically working his belt buckle and lowering his zipper sends a rush of exhilaration through me.

"Daddy's going to put a baby in me," I declare wantonly. "He's going to fill me with his seed until I grow again."

A heavy pant leaves him, and he leans forward to brush my hair off my shoulder, then he places a tender kiss on my bare skin, sucking it for longer than necessary.

His head snaps up, and he glares back at the woman with contempt. "I'm putting a baby in my little pet because this one, I'm keeping." Then he surges forward, taking the wind from my lungs. "She's mine." *Thrust.* The fury behind each powerful grunt is overwhelming, and my fingers tighten around the mirror. "She's fucking mine!" *Slam.* My pussy clenches tightly around him, loving the way he's marking his territory, emphasizing my importance to him and showing her I'm not replaceable. My heart soars and my body simmers with each delectable thrust. "Breed for me, Little Pet. Let me cage you both forever."

I want that.

I want that so bad.

A fire erupts from inside me so strong I burn us both in the process. Warmth spreads through me as I combust around him, and when his teeth sink into my shoulder and he pushes deep inside me, harder than ever, I know he's making his claim.

A permanent one.

Chapter Twenty-Nine

Gracie

Washing my face, I let the water flow over me, having Vinny take me in front of that woman today was hot as hell. Not because I particularly like an audience, more because he was making a point that I am someone he wants in his future, and the way he discussed breeding me set my body alight. Guilt filters through me at the knowledge I have, but I refuse to think about it. My plans are for my daughter's future, not my own.

The way she discussed his basement, a dungeon, has curiosity and jealousy churning my stomach. I feel like I'm being kept from fully satisfying him when other women have willingly handed themselves over to him and he's allowed himself full control of their bodies. Yet with me, he's holding back. I want to be enough for him.

The bathroom door swinging open pulls me from my thoughts, so I wipe the shower window, and a naked Vinny strides in. The confidence this man exudes is all-consuming, his body is a temple of sin, and when he stands at the toilet with his legs parted, my pussy clenches, wishing it was me at his feet.

Holy shit, where the hell did that come from?

My mind flicks back to the contract I signed and the unfamiliar wording of watersports, and though he's not broached the topic with me, I'm suddenly intrigued. Not only do I want to worship this man who gives me his all, I want to give him everything he desires. I don't want to give him any reason to have thoughts about anyone else, not when he has made such a claim on me.

I open the door, and his eyes dart toward mine, heat sparks in his pupils, glaring into my soul, and they flare with a lust so powerful I feel like he's stolen my ability to breathe. Slowly, I lower myself to the shower floor, and his Adam's apple bobs in his throat. The way his shoulder muscles have bunched tight and his cock twitches in his hand has me licking my lips to worship him as he deserves.

"Little Pet," he croons, "I've not finished pissing yet, so I suggest you get up off the floor before I assume you're gifting me with your mouth."

My throat works, and I meet his eyes. "I want to try you."

"Try me?" He crooks an eyebrow.

"Your ..." I gesture toward his dripping cock, and his hand pumps as if not realizing he's jerking himself.

"You want to swallow my piss?"

My cheeks redden and I nod.

"Fuck," he grunts. He stalks toward me, and when he's within reach, he uses the back of his hand to caress my face. "You're a good girl for Daddy; you know that, Little Pet?"

I turn into his touch, then he drops his hand, making me sag.

When he aligns his cock with my face, I steel my shoulders back, then he slowly drags the tip from my forehead to my chin before slapping my cheek with it. "Open your filthy mouth, then, Little Pet."

My lips part, and my jaw falls open. Oh, fuck, why is that so hot? The degradation, the taboo, the submissiveness, and the dominating power behind him have slickness pouring from my pussy. "You're such a little slut for Daddy, isn't that right, Gracie?" Jesus, I love the way he uses my name while he plays with me. Something tells me he didn't do that with the other women, and I relish it.

"Yes, Daddy." I bat my lashes at him, and he hisses through his teeth.

"You're everything I never knew I wanted, Little Pet." He groans, and my heart skyrockets on his words. "Now, stick out your tongue, little slut, and drink Daddy's piss." I do as he asks, and a trickle of warmth splashes onto my tongue. His muscles coil, his stomach contracts, and the veins on his hand protrude.

"That's it, lap up that piss, Little Pet." Using his free hand, he grabs the back of my head and guides my mouth toward his cock. "Drink it fucking down, you hungry little slut, drink what Daddy is gifting you."

The tip of his cock is now in my mouth, and his warm piss floods my throat. I don't know what I expected, but it wasn't this. The feeling of giving him the ultimate control is phenomenal, and pleasure zips through me. Then his fist is working against my chin, and his cock hardens in my mouth, gagging me, but I remain steadfast. As his grip on my head tightens, my scalp pinches, and I struggle to swallow. "Oh, fuck, fuck, I'm going to come on your piss-coated tongue. That's it, little slut. Take Daddy's gift."

I glance up through my tear-soaked lashes and witness the most satisfying sight. His eyes are hooded, his lips parted in awe, and his features are twisted in pleasure as thick ropes of his cum shoot from his cock. A growl erupts from him, and he pulls the tip out and continues to jerk off over my face, down my neck, and over my tits.

"Such a good cum slut for me, Little Pet. All. Fucking. Mine." He swipes the head of his cock down my face, wiping his cum all over me, and I remain kneeling at his feet, feeling more in control and full of love than ever before.

Chapter Thirty

Vinny

My eyes wander over the dinner table, and I take in my family. Rafael looks like he's chewing a fucking wasp as he sits opposite my girl, glaring at a spot above Gracie's head. I'm grateful his wife, Ellie, has the foresight to keep stroking his arm, like she's calming the beast because I'm two seconds away from putting a bullet in my own flesh and blood.

Tommy grins at the end of the table like the cat that got the cream, with Jade beside him swooning at his every word. Rocco leans back in his chair, smirking in my direction with a possessive arm around Hallie's back. His wife is pregnant again, and while I'm grateful, I'm also jealous. Watching my sons experience their wives pregnant with their babies is something I never had the opportunity to experience, and it sends a shooting pain through my chest straight into my heart. I rub over the appendage.

"Heart giving you problems, old man?" Rocco grins.

"Not yet," I clip back.

"Shame, Raf is desperate for that seat." He points toward my chair, and I roll my eyes. His words hold no surprise behind them, it's something we've openly discussed for years now, or at least they have while I sat back and allowed it.

"Are you okay?" Gracie whispers, and my lip twitches at the seriousness in her tone.

I bring her hand to my lips and place a gentle kiss on her soft skin. "I'm fine, baby." Then I lift some of my meat from my plate and place it on hers and use my fork to point at her plate. "Now, eat, I need you to keep your strength up." *Because you might be growing my baby, and I want to keep you healthy.*

"Bonnie is just adorable, Gracie." Hallie smiles toward Bon-Bon, who is frowning at the vegetables on her plate.

"Oh, look, Papa, she looks just like you there when she makes that face," Rocco jokes, and there's a shimmer of glee in his eyes, letting me know he's going to go further. "Get used to it, Gracie. He's a grumpy bastard in his old age." Okay, that wasn't too bad. "Keep popping those blue pills, old man. If you want to keep her, you need to keep up with the young'uns." His words slice through me like ice, and I sit there stunned, but instead of showing him the way his words have affected me, I continue eating in silence and ignore the way Gracie keeps glancing at me like I'm either an invalid or two seconds away from detonating.

Instead, I block out their noise and concentrate on getting through the meal.

DOMINATION

All the while, I imagine the damage I will do on the fucker who impregnated her.

Once through with the meal, I tell the boys I want to speak to them in my office. Rocco groans like I've asked the fucking world of him while Rafael marches ahead of me, not even waiting for me to open my own damn door before relaxing inside.

I asked Hazel to settle my girls down and barely grunted a farewell to my daughters-in-law. Truth be told, as long as they're alive and well, I couldn't give a shit where they are or what they do. I'm only grateful they treated Gracie with the respect she deserves, unlike my oldest son.

I throw open my office door, then slam it behind me. "What the fuck was that?" I demand.

"The pill joke?" Rocco asks, and I pinch the bridge of my nose.

"Not the pill joke," I clip back.

"He's mad at Rafael for barely interacting with Gracie," Tommy states, and my anger dissipates slightly at my son's acknowledgment of his brother's behavior.

Rafael lifts a shoulder. "She's just a little pet, is she not?" His tone is cold and impassive.

"Not!" I bite back. "And you damn well know it."

"Then what is she?"

I want to tell him she's everything, but I don't want them to know she's my weakness, her daughter too, so I choose to settle for something else. "She's not just my little pet," I breathe out, unable to admit my feelings out loud to them.

Rafael rests a foot onto his thigh, and his eyes bounce over my face. "Do you plan on keeping her?"

"Yes," I state. "She's family." I wince, and Rafael picks up on it, his laugh a cruel taunt that sets my teeth on edge.

A heavy sigh leaves me as I drop down into my chair.

"Don't you think it was rather suspect that she just so happens to be the girl that you fucked during the Halloween party, then months later she ends up here needing your help with Robert of all people." I mull over his words.

"He's got a point, Papa," Rocco says.

"What about the baby's father?" Tommy asks, and my spine bolts straight as they talk about Bonnie, the little girl who has captured my heart. "Who is he?"

"It doesn't matter. She's mine," I snipe out, meaning every damn word.

"There you go again." Rafael gestures. "Make up your mind, old man, they're either yours or they're not."

"She's young," I say.

Rocco's face softens, and it's the first time my youngest son has shown this side of him outside of his own small family unit. "I was only joking about the pills and shit, Papa. I know your cock works fine, seen it enough fucking times," he jokes, attempting to lighten the mood.

Rafael stands and buttons up his jacket. "We need answers before you do anything rash like propose, or worse, fucking knock her up," he grunts. "Just fucking wrap it up until I have news. Maybe Robert will sing like a fucking canary when we torture him." He smirks, and something tells me he isn't wrong about any of it.

She's keeping things from me, and I wonder if it's to do with Bonnie's biological father. A much-younger man, one she can have more of a future with than I could ever offer.

Gracie

Something happened at dinner, and Vinny has shut down. He'd normally follow me to bed soon after I feed Bonnie so he can have that part of me too.

My gut twists as I consider if it's something I have done. The way in which Rafael glared at me lets me know he doesn't approve of my existence, and who can blame him? It's almost like he can see straight through me. All my secrets exposed to him. Does he realize I will break his father's heart when he's trusted me to treasure it?

Will he hate me for what I'm about to do?

Lying in the darkness, I don't know what time Vinny slips into bed, but when he does, he positions his cock at my entrance and slides inside with a deep sigh, with his arm banding around me. I lower my lips to his tattooed bicep and gift him a kiss. "Something's upset you," I whisper into the night. "Is it me?"

"No," he responds.

"Then what is it?" I turn to face him while remaining pinned by his cock, but I wouldn't have it any other way.

He exhales, but when he lifts his eyes to meet mine, there's vulnerability there that I want to banish. "I don't like Rocco referring to me as being too old for you." My mind flicks through the conversation at the dinner table. "He insinuated someone younger was better for you," he adds for more clarity. My feelings for him twist like knives. He's hurting, and it's because of my very presence.

"I don't want anyone younger. I want you," I say, then I rest my head on his chest while he raises his arm behind his head to prop it up, enabling him to glance down on me. Feeling his warm, solid body beneath mine sends a flurry of protectiveness through me. Happiness sets sail, and for the first time in my life, I feel like I'm home despite being so far from there.

"Hmm ..." He flicks his gaze down at me. "I don't like the thoughts of me holding you back, Gracie," he admits, making my heart squeeze in my chest.

I shake my head, and my hair sways over him. "You're not. Someone younger couldn't be my daddy." I bite into my lip to stop myself from smiling.

"What about Bonnie's father?" he asks.

My blood turns to ice, and he raises his eyebrow as if aware of my reaction. "Wh-what about him?" I squeak.

"Your father said he was young." His lips turn up in a sneer, and the vein protrudes on his neck, like it's taking everything in him to refrain from poking further.

It feels like I can't control the blood racing around my body as panic sets in.

Our gazes remain locked, and I choose my next words careful, as to not anger him further. "He isn't in the picture."

"And if he was?"

I hold his stare, hoping he can see the truth in my eyes, in my very soul. "I want you."

His shoulders relax and his cock twitches. "How much do you want me, Little Pet."

"So much," I pant, and the intensity between us switches to something more.

"Come up here and straddle my face, I want to taste you." He taps my ass.

"You know what I taste like." I grin, and he lifts me from his cock and positions me over his face.

"Oh, I think you're mistaken, Little Pet. Daddy needs to taste all of you." He licks his lips for emphasis, and a flush of arousal flashes through me. Oh, god, he wants to ... "Let me lick the piss from my little pet." Holy shit. My eyes widen and my pussy clenches.

Before I know what's happening, he's holding my ass in place with one hand while pressing on my lower stomach with the other, forcing a squirt of pee to leave me. My mouth falls open in horror, but as I stare into his dark eyes, all I see reflecting back at me is total possession. He owns me, commands every inch of me, and if he wants to take my piss, he will, no matter what. "Hold on to the headboard and watch yourself piss on your daddy while he licks his little pet's pussy clean."

I almost fall forward, overcome with stimulation. His filthy words, the degrading act, the tremendous feeling of wanting to please him while desperate for him to get off on the fact he commands me, have me gripping onto the headboard. I force myself past my self-imposed limitations and give in to deliver a warm stream of piss over his face.

"Oh, god!" I cry out, in part mortification, but I glance over my shoulder to see him working his solid cock furiously, and the way his abs contract like he's struggling to rein in the control has me removing one hand to pump my aching full breast.

"Oh, fuck, Gracie." His face twists and his warm mouth covers my pussy, then I push down on him and a feral groan erupts from inside him as he swallows me down. A flick of his tongue has me following behind with my own orgasm, leaving me a panting mess covered in milk.

One thing's for sure, I don't know how I'm going to leave my daddy.

And worse, I don't want to.

Chapter Thirty-One

Gracie

After the usual breakfast routine of me suckling on Vinny, then him feeding me like I'm incapable, he ordered me to go shower. When I got out of the shower, he was waiting to brush my hair and dress me in clothes of his choice. He even left a soft-pink nail polish on my dresser that he ordered specifically for me to paint my toes. Apparently, he likes the innocence of the color.

I got Bonnie dressed, then knocked on his office door, and he settled us on his lap like we weighed nothing while continuing to make demands about shipments on his phone. Once he finished, he informed me I was spending the day with Hazel at a church community center. To say I was delighted was an understatement. He praised me for being a good girl while he fawned over how adorable Bonnie looked with the little pink ribbon in her hair that he purchased for her to match her pink flamingo-themed dress.

"How are you getting along?" Hazel asks as I pack another sachet of oatmeal into the box. We're packing food for the underprivileged, and the prospect of doing something meaningful for someone else feels amazing, a buzz of exhilaration flows through me at knowing I'm helping to make a difference.

"I'm loving it here. Thank you so much for suggesting this to Vinny." My gaze lands on Bonnie on the play mat with another little girl not much older than her. Both of them are stuffing building blocks into their mouths.

"He just wants you to be happy." She smiles, and my heart twists as I consider never seeing her again.

I move my focus away from her, hoping she can't see the guilt I feel from head to toe. "I appreciate everything he's doing for me and Bonnie, and I appreciate you too, thank you, Hazel." I give her hand a squeeze.

"Dare I say he loves you and that little girl." She tilts her head toward Bonnie, and I fight back the tears threatening to spill.

"Gracie, is that really you?" A familiar voice has me spinning to face the guy I've not seen in around eighteen months, right before my father stopped me from going to church.

"Matthew?"

My gaze roams over him. He's taller than I remember, or maybe he grew. His dark hair is longer, and he has more muscle than before. He blushes and shifts from foot to foot. "Yeah." He laughs awkwardly, then clears his throat. "What happened to you?"

DOMINATION

"My father, he didn't like me going to church," I admit, embarrassment coloring my features.

His eyes narrow. "What?"

"I know." I roll my eyes.

"I knew it was him that had stopped you coming." His jaw tightens before he blows out a deep breath. "Well, I'm pleased you're here now. I go around all the churches in the area, collecting the donations and delivering them." He gestures toward the boxes.

Hazel steps to the side, and her focus lands on Matthew. "Gracie, are you going to introduce me?"

"Oh. I'm so sorry." I shake my head. "This is Matthew Bardwell, a friend from where I lived with my father." Her gaze ping-pongs between us before she glances over her shoulder toward Bonnie, making my spine steel straight at the thoughts that must be running through her mind. I step in front of Bonnie to block his view of her. The last thing I want is questions from him that causes her to report back to Vinny when I'm so close to freedom.

"Everything okay here?" Massio asks, stepping between Matthew and me.

I tilt my head up to take him in. "Yes, everything is fine. He's just asking if I need any help with the boxes." I gesture toward the boxes while Matthew continues to eye me skeptically. My eyes implore his, and he nods before stepping toward the table housing the boxes, but Massio snaps his arm out across Matthew's chest. "I got this, kid," he grunts with a wink, and Matthew shrinks away from us. While I continue loading the boxes up with goodies, my mind wanders with thoughts of my plans flittering away. I need to make a move, and soon, before Vinny puts a stop to my outings and before my feelings of guilt and love grow to the point of no return. If I open up to him, there's no way he will ever let us leave, and this might be our only chance of true freedom.

Chapter Thirty-Two

Vinny

"What the fuck do you mean some punk was chatting her up?" I sneer toward Massio.

"I didn't say that. I said he offered to carry her boxes."

"Carry her fucking boxes?" I pace the room while flitting from pinching the bridge of my nose to dragging a hand through my hair. "Is that what they call it these days?"

"I think you're blowing all of this out of proportion, sir."

An irritated scoff leaves me, and I deliver another swift kick to the lifeless piece of shit on the basement floor.

"Did Bonnie look like him?" I snap my eyes toward Massio, and he shifts on his feet.

He grimaces and my chest tightens. "Sir, Bonnie looks like Gracie."

I couldn't agree more, she's her double, but she has to

have some of her biological father's DNA in her. "Yes. But did she look like the punk?"

He sighs heavily, and irritations zips up my spine. "I don't know." He shrugs. "It wasn't at the forefront of my mind."

Wasn't at the forefront of his fucking mind? "Remind me what the fuck I pay you for?" I snap.

Massio stiffens and his glare darkens. "For security, and that's exactly what I was doing. I checked to see if he posed a risk, and he didn't. Jesus, Vinny, you need to get a fucking handle on this jealousy, it's not like you." He's not wrong, I feel out of control, my mind spiraling that she's going to take Bonnie, leave, and never look back, all for a younger guy who gave her daughter life.

"Take your aggression out on him." He gestures toward the piece of shit on the floor. "We'll catch up later when you've calmed down." He spins on his boots and heads out the door, slamming it so damn loud vibrations work through the room. Barely giving him a chance to leave, I unzip my pants.

Chapter Thirty-Three

Gracie

It's been two weeks since I started going to the church community center, and I live for it.

As soon as I settle Bonnie, I head down the stairs. I haven't seen Vinny all day, only a single text message telling me he will be home late. Hazel will be in bed by now, so I creep through the house. Ever since my encounter with that vile woman at the store, all I can think about is her taunting me with the basement that I've never been taken to. A dungeon she called it, even the sound of it is terrifying.

A chill sweeps over me as I tiptoe through the kitchen and down the corridor I've never been. Then darkness engulfs me, causing me to swallow back the fear gathered in my throat. What if he has someone in that room right now? What if he keeps me in the house and a woman in there? Yet a voice niggles inside me, asking me why I care; I plan on leaving anyway.

As I shove open the door, I pull my shoulders back. Maybe this is what I need to give me the push to leave when I have one foot out the door. My footing wavers on the first step, but I continue on, ignoring the way I tremble as I descend the stairs. When I reach the bottom, there's a small corridor and a door leading off both ends, so I decide to turn right first.

My breath stills as I push open the heavy door and step inside. It's a bedroom, a luxurious one, and stepping further inside, I see it's used primarily for sex. There're hooks above the bed and cuffs on the bedposts. To my right is a strange see-through wall, with a mirror behind it, and to my left is a large white leather chair resembling a throne. On the wall is a huge television screen. Arousal seeps from me as I slowly take in all the contraptions and instruments attached to the hanging chains.

A throat clears behind me, making me jump, and I spin to face Vinny. "What are you doing down here, Little Pet?" He raises his eyebrow while wiping his hands on a rag, making me wonder what he's been doing.

"You've never brought me down here," I state.

"Should I have?"

I glance around the room again, taking in the abundance of sex toys sitting on a shelf on the wall beside the mirror.

"That woman at the store told me about it."

His jaw tics and his fists ball as he throws the rag to the floor. "And what did she say?"

"Nothing, really." I shrug. "I was just curious why you hadn't brought me down here."

Before I know what's happening, he's behind me

DOMINATION

sweeping my hair off my shoulder to place a kiss on the bare skin of my neck. I sway as his scent encompasses me and revel in the way he bands a protective arm around my stomach, holding me in place. His free hand curls around my throat, toying with the collar, and my panties dampen under his dominance.

"I've not thought about this room since you've been here, if you want to play, we can play in your bedroom." I bend my head to the side as he kisses up and down my neck, causing a flurry of excitement to shoot through me.

My chest rises higher with each kiss, the way his thick palm caresses my stomach has arousal seeping from me. I close my eyes, imagining his fingers slipping a little bit lower to take the ache off. "What if I want to play here?" I breathe out.

He detaches himself from me, and my body sags at losing his warmth. "What is it you want to do, Gracie?" he huffs like he's annoyed at my words.

Everything, I want to tell him, but I'm terrified he'll refuse me.

"What you do with other women," I admit, and follow his retreating form toward the chair.

He drops down into it and stretches his legs wide while he runs a finger over his lips. The silence between us is brutal, and I can hear my heart pounding in my ears.

What if he refuses, rejects me?

I lick my lips, and he his eyes follow the action.

He exudes confidence and control. Pure dominance shines in his eyes, making me nervous but intrigued as my gaze flits around the room.

Eventually, he sighs heavily. "Over there is the medical cabinet." He gestures toward a cabinet.

"Medical cabinet?" I scrunch my nose. Why on earth would he need a medical cabinet? Unless he hurts his pets.

He shakes his head in such a way it's like he's hearing my spiraling thoughts. "It houses things like laxatives to clear out a pet's ass, pain relief for after impact play, condoms in case I want to switch between ass and pussy, ointment, lotions, and lubes. There's also liquid ecstasy for enhancing a woman's sex drive. Then over there"—he points toward a dark corner of the room, and my gaze follows—"is a cage, Gracie. An actual cage for when I want my pet locked up."

My pulse races, and I use my hand to cover my heart. "I normally fuck more than one pet at any given time, so I'd have one in the cage begging to be let out, begging for me to fuck her while I take another." His words are laced in shame, and I hate that more than I hate what he's told me. Surprisingly, the only thing I feel is jealousy. If he thought this would put me off, he's wrong.

"I don't want to share you," I admit. "I don't want you to fuck other women, Daddy," I say louder this time.

"Trust me, I don't want to fuck other women either." His eyes lock with mine, and I see the sincerity behind his words, and hope spears me to my core.

When he opens his mouth, I hang on every word. "Strip and bend over the bed." His husky voice sounds almost detached, but excitement gathers in my center at the prospect of pleasing him.

Methodically, I disrobe, loving the way his pupils

darken. Then I saunter over to the bed and bend over, resting my face on the mattress. With my feet still on the ground, I wait with heightened expectation. From the corner of my eye, I watch him go over to the shelf, and my pussy clenches as he selects something. I can't make out what he's carrying, but when he steps up behind me, every cell in my body is alive with anticipation coupled with need.

"Please, Daddy," I whimper, unable to help myself.

"You've been a bad girl, Little Pet."

I clutch the silk sheets.

"Do you remember your safe word?"

"I won't need it," I pant with confidence, determined to take whatever he gives me.

A loud chuckle bounces off the walls. "Tell me what it is," he says, trailing a finger down my spine, leaving goose bumps in its wake.

"Red."

The air is electric between us.

"Bad little pets get their asses ruined." I jolt at his words, and without warning, there's a sound in the air I don't recognize before a sharp throb of pain on my ass cheek makes me cry out. Without giving me time to adjust to the deep aching pain, there's another, then another. Each makes my ass throb and my pussy clench as I scream out. "Fuck, that's it, scream, Little Pet. Let Daddy hear those tears while you take his paddle."

A paddle? Wetness slips between my legs caused by the sharp thwack of pain against my ass and the pure dominance flowing from Vinny.

My tears flow freely. I'm unable to hold them back,

with each smack to my ass causing a fresh sob as I tremble beneath him, completely submissive, my clit aching with need. So much so I rub myself against the sheets, hoping to receive some gratification.

"Fuck, you look good, Little Pet. Keep crying, keep crying for your daddy." I realize now that he wants to break me, he wants me to plead for him so he can care for me after. He gets off on the pain of my cries as much as he gets off on the way he cares for me like no other, and before now, the sadist in him had been absent.

He grips my hair and pulls me to my feet, the rough handling catching me off guard. "Up! On your knees."

I move quickly, almost stumbling over my own feet to fall to the floor at his command. "Open those lips, stretch your mouth around this thick cock."

My lips part, and my eyes widen when a silicone cock is thrust between my lips, forcing me to gag. "That's it, Little Pet, suck that cock like a needy slut." His hips thrust forward with each pump of the cock, as though it's his I'm taking. "This cock has been molded to match my own, look how you drool around it, Little Pet. So eager for Daddy's cock you're practically drooling over a silicone one." He stares down at me through hooded eyes with such intensity I whimper around the object, delighting in the way his own cock tents his pants.

He withdraws the cock from my mouth, and a stream of spittle follows it, making him chuckle. "Up!" He grips my arm and pulls me to my feet, and I wince at the bite of pain behind the action. His rough handling of me is foreign but not unwanted. In fact, I crave it.

"Stand against the wall." He points toward the clear

wall, and my eyes knit together, unsure of what the wall is used for, but I do as he asks.

He follows behind me, each step causes my ass to throb, then he shocks the hell out of me by slamming the cock against the wall and only now do I realize it's suctioned. "Give me your hands." He holds his palm out for me, and I don't even think to ask why, I simply do as he asks. He restrains me with cuffs attached to a chain on a hook above me. "I'm going to fuck your ass with that"—he tilts his head toward the suctioned cock—"while I bury my cock in your slick little cunt."

He's what?

"I'm going to fuck my baby into you while I stuff you with my cocks, Gracie." He smirks.

Panic lances through my chest as my gaze bounces back and forth from the silicone cock to him.

He presses a button on the wall I hadn't noticed until now, and slowly, I'm being lifted off the floor as horror fills my bloodstream for the first time since setting foot in here.

Holy shit, I'm being suspended.

"Wrap your legs around my waist, and I'll make sure that cock doesn't hurt you too much, Gracie." There's the familiar tenderness in his tone while using my given name, and I wrap my legs around his waist, melting as my muscles relax. "Good girl." He nuzzles into my neck, and I swoon at his touch, my muscles becoming like putty in his strong hands.

"Let Daddy play with this pussy, then we're going to fuck you at the same time." His eyes are ablaze with desire, and I could swim in it. My only response is to nod.

His fingers swirl over my throbbing bud, and I bite my lip to stop myself from coming too soon. "Fuck, you're so wet already, Little Pet. You make Daddy so proud." While his wet fingers slide around to my ass to coat my hole in my arousal, he kisses down my neck, then scrapes his teeth over the spot, and I moan in satisfaction. The tip of his finger toys with my entrance, and he pushes it inside my ass. In and out, in and out. "That's a good girl."

Then he removes his finger, and I feel the hard prod at my ass. I freeze, remembering it being painful the last time. "Shhh, let Daddy's big cock inside you, like a good little pet," he coaxes, pressing on my swollen nub, and I moan.

The sound of his belt buckle has my body falling lax, the tip of the silicone cock pushes against my asshole while I feel the tip of his cock at my pussy. "Please."

The cuffs bite into my wrists, and I push my chest against him, begging for his touch, begging for a release of any kind.

"Jesus," he grunts, and steps forward, forcing my ass back onto the cock. Pain burns through me, and he slams his lips down on my neck while pushing up inside me with his cock at the same time the dildo burns through me. Sensation overload lances through me, the pain, the tenderness, and the pleasure force me to orgasm. He takes this as his opportunity to sink both cocks inside me, and I feel like my body is being split in half. "Take it," he growls into my neck. "Take those thick cocks, little slut."

I tug on the chains and cry out. My body is on fire, roaring with the heat of his possession all around me. The strangled sound of my wail bounces off the room, and with it, his hips piston in and out of me at an erratic speed. Thrust after thrust, sear after sear, my ass and pussy are pounded while I hang from the chain in beautiful torment.

A heavy feeling is building inside me, and I welcome it. The sounds of our panting breaths and skin slapping against one another are erotic, euphoric, and add to my impending orgasm.

When his teeth sink into the flesh of my neck, I scream in glorious agony, so overwhelmed black spots consume me, and I freefall into the abyss.

Chapter Thirty-Four

Vinny

F uck me, she's incredible. I stroke the hair from her face as I watch her sleeping form. After coming inside her, I tucked my cock in my pants, lowered her from the wall, then carried her through he house, hoping I didn't bump into any of my staff along the way.

Watching her take the cock in her ass through the mirror was sensational. The feeling of her holes full with my cock had possessiveness rushing rampantly around my veins.

Since she's crept into my heart, I find the thought of anyone seeing her naked but me almost unbearable. Which is absurd, given I previously took great pleasure in parading my little pets around my home, then fucked them in every position possible, audience be damned.

The way she embraced my darker side is reassuring, but the thought of that bitch Cindy making her feel inadequate has poison flooding my veins. My little pet is perfect. I toy with the strands of her silky hair, placing another kiss on her shoulder.

After moisturizing her bruised ass, I took time taking caring of every inch of her. Of course, this meant shoving the cum that escaped her pussy deep inside her. Then I painted her lips with the remnants, all while I whispered to her how treasured she is and willed my baby to take form inside her.

My phone buzzes from my nightstand, annoying the fuck out of me, but as I reach over to answer, my blood turns to ice. It's Rafael, and he wouldn't call me in the middle of the night unless it was urgent. Gracie is still out cold, so I place it on speaker while I slip my cock inside her hole once again, then bring her heavy tit to my lips.

It's not lost on me that I'm about to feed from my girl while I'm speaking to my son, but I don't give a shit. I have needs, something I'm sure my son understands.

"Go on," I drawl, and her milk bubbles out of her nipple.

"Robert left the rehab center two days ago." My mouth stills above her nipple as fury lances through me. "Don't worry, I had some guys pick him up at his old house." My muscles relax, and I take a pull of her milk, the taste on my tongue soothing. "We've delivered him to the warehouse as instructed."

"Good," I grunt out, my hips moving of their own accord, delivering deep, powerful thrusts.

"I'm going to go home now and sink inside my woman. I'll see you tomorrow."

DOMINATION

"I want answers from him tomorrow. He doesn't die until I have them," I grunt my response.

"You'll have your answers tomorrow, trust me, Papa."

His words settle me, and I end the call determined to spend the rest of the night worshipping my comatose little pet.

Chapter Thirty-Five

Gracie

My body aches like hell, but it's delicious and not the kind of ache from a cruel punishment but one forged in love. I can still smell the peach soothing balm on my skin that Vinny applied during the night. Small pieces of the night flit through my mind, and I'm unable to decide if I dreamed them or not. I think Vinny received a call, and I'm sure it was discussing my father, but I must be mistaken, he'd have at least mentioned it to me if it was. He fucked me slowly like he was worshipping my body and fed from me while he spoke. I touch my breasts, and they're not as heavy as they were before I went down to the basement, but my mind is at war with myself, and nausea rushes through me.

Oh, holy hell, the basement. No wonder I'm so sore today. My cheeks flush as I consider the two cocks that stretched me wide open to the point of pain.

Pleasure took over me, and I fell into a dark, euphoric subspace I've only read about, one of pure bliss.

"Oh, god." I palm my face and head toward the bathroom to freshen up, trying my best to ignore the sickness rolling in my stomach as a memory from last night infiltrates my head, *"You'll have your answers tomorrow, trust me, Papa."* My father is in rehab, I know he is. Vinny would tell me if he wasn't. It was a dream, it had to be.

After showering and freshening up, I head down the stairs, disappointed he's already at the breakfast room table when I step inside. His jaw locks, and the glare behind his eyes is seething, so I step back, unsure of what brought this response on from him.

He shakes his head, then holds out his hand. "Don't be alarmed, Little Pet. It's me I'm angry with." My eyebrows furrow. "Come." I slip my hand into his, and he pulls me onto his lap. I wince at the tenderness of my ass hitting his leg, and he chuckles, causing me to narrow my eyes at him.

"I don't want you naked around the house anymore." I lift my head to face him, hating the way he chastises me. "I don't want anyone else to see you like this but me." He cradles my face in the palms of his hands, and the warmth of his touch burrows beneath my skin, setting my heart alight, much like a torch. The darkness in his eyes suddenly looks lighter than ever. "You're mine, Little Pet. My Gracie." His words scorch my soul, burning through me with such strength the air is stolen from my lungs. The truth behind his words is more than I could ever wish for. "You're mine," he repeats, and tears fill my eyes. "Am I yours?" he rasps.

DOMINATION

My heart kicks in my chest as I lick my lips, and he waits with bated breath for my response. Can I do this? Can I give up my dream for freedom, Bonnie's too? But to what expense, that of a man who loves us unconditionally. Surely that brings more security and love than any freedom can offer. "You're mine," I whisper, and he exhales loudly.

A knock on the door interrupts us, and Vinny jumps up from his chair and places me on it, then he blocks me from view.

"You ready, sir?" Massio asks without so much as giving me a second glance.

Vinny brushes a hand through his hair. "Yeah, gimme a minute."

Massio closes the door behind him, and Vinny shrugs off his suit jacket. Before I know what's happening, he's pushing my arms through the sleeves. "We'll discuss this later." He waves a hand over my body, then takes my chin between his fingers. "I've asked you before to use a robe. I mean it, Gracie; you might be my little pet, but I don't want anyone else to benefit from that. You make me possessive as hell." He chuckles to himself and shakes his head, then blows out a deep breath like it's annoying.

"Yes, Daddy." I smile, trying to fight back the smirk on my lips.

He licks his lips, and his eyes darken. "You're my world, Little Pet, and I never want to lose you." He drags the back of his fingers down my cheek. "If I could cage you forever, I would," he murmurs. My heart stutters; doesn't he see? His house is a cage, albeit a luxurious one, but a cage no less.

He clears his throat, and his hand falls away from my face. "I shouldn't be home late tonight, why don't you wait up and we can have dinner together?" He glances outside. "On the patio," he tacks on.

"Like a date?" Hope springs in my chest, and his laugh rumbles.

"I guess so. I'll see you later, be a good girl." He places a soft kiss on my head, strokes my hair, then leaves.

As soon as the door clicks shut, I feel a vibration against my chest, making me jump, and I slap my hand against it. "Shoot." I dig into Vinny's jacket pocket, realizing it's his phone, and when I glance down at the message, it's like ice has slid into my veins, invading my bloodstream.

The words dance on the screen as I blink and attempt to concentrate on what they say.

> Rafael: I have Robert here waiting to spill his secrets.

Panic floods me, my head becomes woozy, and my entire body trembles. Spill his secrets? They have my father.

"You'll have your answers tomorrow, trust me, Papa." It wasn't a dream last night.

My eyes flick toward the door, and I hear the heavy thud of Vinny's footsteps approaching, so I shove the phone back in his pocket while I remain dumbstruck at what I just read.

The door swings open, and I startle. Vinny strides toward me, and I shrink back on my chair. "Did I make you jump?" he asks. "I'm sorry, I forgot my phone." He leans over me and slides his hand into his jacket pocket to retrieve his phone. "Got it." He winks before heading toward the door. The moment it clicks behind him, I release a breath.

We need to leave, and soon, because when Vinny finds out the truth, he will know I betrayed him, then there's no going back.

I'll be caged forever.

Chapter Thirty-Six

Vinny

My blood pumps with adrenaline. Fuck, I can't wait to deal with this scumbag. It's been years in the making, and finally, fucking finally, I have the perfect excuse to rid the world of the pathetic lowlife that is Robert Kennedy.

Massio slides open the warehouse door, and my eyes find Rocco sitting on a crate cleaning his nails with the damn knife he never lets out of his sight. My son has a thing for blood play, and after witnessing the cuts on his wife, I'd have a guess that it spills over into his bedroom too.

"Nice of you to join us." Rafael raises a critical eyebrow in my direction, and if I wasn't in my fifties, I would flip him the bird.

"Papa takes longer to get out of bed in the morning, isn't that right, Papa?" Rocco taunts while speaking obnoxiously loudly.

Massio chuckles, and the moment my gaze slices to his, he slams his mouth shut.

"He's just coming 'round." Tommy gives Robert a swift kick that has him howling like a bitch. The man looks barely able to hold his head, and I smile at the way my boys have worked him over. Blood oozes from his nose, his lip is split, and his shirt is bloody and sliced up, telling me Rocco has already started on his torture.

The chain he clings onto is stretching his arms to capacity, and I have to hand it to my boys, they know what they're doing.

"Did Daddy get his milk and cookies before leaving this morning?" Rocco's eyebrows dance with jest, and this time I slap the back of his head.

"Shut the fuck up, that's your future stepmother you're talking about."

"Fucking great. You're barely here most of the time already," Rafael chastises, and I sneer in his direction. I've dedicated enough of my fucking life to the Mafia. If I want to slow down, then I fucking will, especially now that I have a reason to.

Rafael steps forward. "You need to take a look at what we discovered when we located him." He holds out his phone to me, and I take it.

Slowly, I take in what I'm seeing. A dark room with a mattress on the floor with one thin sheet and a crib beside it. "It's the basement. Seems like he kept her there."

Anger.

Fury.

Utter rage burns beneath my skin.

A deep hue of violent red surges inside me, blocking the light from my eyes.

He kept them in a fucking basement.

What the actual fuck?

"Keep going." He gestures toward the phone, and my thumb shakes as I swipe onto the next image showing a door with a padlock.

My legs threaten to buckle. I don't know what's more shocking, seeing these images or my reaction to them.

I've seen some serious fucked-up shit before now, but nothing, and I mean nothing, has drawn this reaction from me.

"He locked the basement door. They were practically prisoners," Rafael continues, and all I can think about is how I'm going to destroy him bit by fucking bit.

Prisoners?

My beautiful girls were treated so cruelly.

A voracious anger takes over me, and my nostrils flare as every muscle in my body coils at what Rafael is telling me. I swipe along to the next one, a lock on the refrigerator. He locked the fucking refrigerator? No wonder she ate so little when she first came to me.

My blood boils and the fury inside me feels like no other. The only time I have ever felt like this is when one of the bitches I married tried to harm Rocco.

All of her vulnerability that bleeds from her makes sense now—the lack of clothes, the being grateful for the smallest of items.

She had next to nothing. Hell, she didn't even have a bed.

"There's no records of her going to school either, or

healthcare," Rafael adds, and I snap my focus to him. Her struggle to work through the contract dances at the forefront of my mind, her struggle at the restaurant. Can my beautiful girl not read? I rub at the pain in my chest. Worse than any of this, she didn't tell me.

Concern mars his features. "She had nothing, Papa." His tone is full of sympathy, not something Rafael is accustomed to.

Pure unadulterated anger bleeds from my every pore, and I lunge toward Robert with savage intent. Rafael is quick to pull me back, but I attempt to shrug off my son, conscious not to harm him.

"We'll make the fucker pay," Tommy seethes, tugging the fucker's head back by his hair, and my muscles slowly unfurl.

"Damn fucking straight we will." Rocco springs up from the crate, his eyes alight with retribution.

A callous laugh causes the hairs on the back of my neck to rise, and Tommy releases Robert's head, allowing him to stare back at me. The malice and cruelty are evident on his face, and not a trace of his daughter's attributions are there. Has he always looked so deranged?

He swallows. "I almost had you. Almost." He shakes his head. "I set this up a long time ago."

"What the fuck are you talking about?" Rocco bellows.

"The Halloween party," Rafael states, ten steps ahead of our thoughts. Yet more proof my son is the perfect man for the position of don.

"Right." He sniffles, and that move tells me he's withdrawing again. "The *family* Halloween party. Party of

DOMINATION

the fucking century," he sneers, like a green-eyed monster. "I sent her in there. The little fucking princess desperate for acceptance, a desperate little whore. I could have gotten good money for her, you know?" My fists pump beside me, and my sons glance toward me with concern, but I stare ahead at the piece of shit who dared to treat her with such disrespect. "I told her she needed to fuck you, and she did it." I jolt at his words, and pain slices through me, cutting so deep it's almost impossible to remain standing. Yet, somehow, I do. I can only put it down to my training. His words feel like the ultimate betrayal. Would she have ever slept with me if it wasn't for following his command?

"What are you talking about? Why the fuck would you want her to fuck him?" Tommy asks as his eyes bounce over his face searching for a lie. He won't find one, I can feel it in my heart as a piece of it crumbles. She fucked me as a plan, and while I know her actions after were not part of her plan because I simply gave her no choice, I can't help but feel the betrayal deep in my soul.

She lied.

My heart squeezes, and a sound similar to a whimper leaves me.

All this time, she lied.

"I needed leverage." He spits out some blood on the concrete floor.

"Leverage?" Tommy queries as my gut twists. "What kind of fucking leverage?"

"Her compliance." He grins manically.

My phone rings, and I pull it from my pocket to silence it, but seeing Hazel's name on the screen has something akin to panic settling in my stomach. "Hazel?" I snap.

"She's gone, Vincent."

My world spins, and I struggle to register what she's saying. "What?"

"Gracie, she went to the restroom, but now she's gone." She sniffles, and I want to tell her to stop with the dramatics, but I need answers, and quick. "Bonnie too."

She ran. I feel it deep in my gut, and it cuts deep. She ran, she fucking left me.

My lungs feel like they're collapsing as I try but fail to remain calm.

My head spins, and I feel like I'm floating into the unknown. *What the fuck is happening to me?*

Warm hands turn my face toward his, and Rocco's eyes come into view through a hazy blur. "Papa, concentrate." He nods toward my phone, forcing me out of my head. "Calm down and concentrate." His eyes drill into mine, and I give my son a swift nod.

"I'll be there soon." I end the call and face my sons, then clear my throat to wipe away the emotion. "Gracie and Bonnie are missing."

A laugh erupts from the piece of shit. "Well, look at that, she did it after all." He grins.

"Did what, motherfucker?" Rocco surges toward him, his eyes alight with brutality.

"She's starting over." He smiles sadistically, exposing his bloodied teeth.

A phone ringing cuts through the air, and Rafael's spine straightens as he presses on his phone. My body stills, something inside me telling me to remain on the spot.

"Ellie, now's not a good ti—"

"Rafael, you need to get out of the warehouse. Right fucking now! You're about to be raided." Ellie's shriek is loud and hysterical and clear as fucking day, even without the speaker on.

"What?"

"Darryl Davis messaged me. He says you're all about to be raided, please just leave."

"Darryl fucking Davis?" Even I can hear the jealousy slithering through him.

"Don't ask me to explain now, just do it," she urges.

Tommy is already lowering Robert, and the fucker thrashes about, attempting to get free.

Rafael springs into action, barking orders for the drugs and weapons to be concealed. Rocco is rushing Robert out the back door, and Tommy is pushing the bags of guns into the metal trap door. Massio helps lock down the warehouse, and the chaos of everyone around me has me frozen to the spot. For the first time in my life, I don't want to put our Mafia life first.

I want to choose her.

"Papa?" I snap my gaze up to meet Rafael's stern expression. "Go find her." He stares at me with concern shining in his eyes.

I swallow the knot in my throat and admit what I don't want to admit. "That's not how this life works, son."

"Says who? You're the Mafia don, write your own fucking rules." His eyes implore mine. "I know I will."

His lip curls into a smile, and he flicks his head toward the door. "Go."

Pride takes over me. The son I've raised, the man I trained to one day become leader, is exactly who I wish I could be.

I give Rafael a firm nod, and the tension slips from his face, then he spins and continues barking orders at his brothers.

"Massio, let's go!" Without giving it another thought, I rush toward the door knowing damn well things are about to change forever.

Chapter Thirty-Seven

Gracie

Felix was our protection for today, and he took us to the community center. Throughout the entire car journey, I could feel Hazel's eyes on me, watching, scrutinizing as to why I was so quiet. I was going through the motions, hiding my true intent with barely held restraint. A thin thread threatening to snap at any moment, but I couldn't allow it, not when there was so much at stake.

Once we arrived, I made drinks as usual and gave Felix his. Guilt lances through me as he takes sip after sip.

After Vinny left this morning, I hatched a plan to distract our chaperone today, and everything else was already in place. I never expected following through with it would be so difficult. I thought I'd be excited at the prospect of getting what I always wanted, but instead, I feel the pointed end of a blade digging into my heart at the thought of losing the man I've grown to love.

Felix takes another sip of the coffee laced with the laxatives from Vinny's dungeon, and I close my eyes as I imagine never seeing him again. A tear slips down my cheek, and I swipe it away. It doesn't matter how I feel about him; he will hate me when he finds out the truth.

"Are you okay, honey, you're awfully quiet today?" Hazel asks, scanning me as she places another tin of fruit into the box.

I clear my throat. "Hazel, would you mind lending me some money please?"

She rears back before her features soften. "Sure, hun, but can I ask what for?"

"I want to buy Vinny a thank-you gift." I swallow back the lie before continuing on. "For letting us stay with him."

She pats my hand and giggles. "You really are a sweetie. He wouldn't want anything." She shakes her head, and panic ripples through me. "But I think he'd love the gesture. I don't think he's ever received a gift before." My heart twists on her words, so I close my eyes momentarily to distract myself from the trauma of what I'm about to do.

She reaches beneath the table and grabs her purse, then she slides fifty dollars into my hand, closing my palm around it.

Her gaze suddenly catches onto something over my shoulder. "Oh, dear lord, you don't look so good, Felix."

I glance over my shoulder to witness Felix holding his stomach. He winces, then darts toward the restroom.

This is it; this is the moment that's going to change our lives.

DOMINATION

The moment we're free.

So why does the anxiety thrumming through my veins make it feel like the ultimate betrayal? And why does my heart feel like it's being torn from my chest as I stroll toward Bonnie with one thing in mind?

Freedom.

Chapter Thirty-Eight

Vinny

Savage rage has me pushing the little punk up against the community center office door. "P-p-please sir, I d-don't know anything, I swear." The smell of urine fills my nostrils, but it's not my own, so of course my dick doesn't twitch as I stare him down, and disgust rolls off me.

"You fucked my girl, don't act dumb, you sad sack little fucker. I'm about to destroy every inch of you." He pales even more than before, if that's humanly possible.

"I-I didn't," he cries, literal tears streaming down his face. "I swear. It wasn't me." He splutters between swiping at the snot dripping from his nose. My lip curls in distaste. Did she really fuck this kid? I scratch my head with the handgun I'm holding. It makes no sense, none at all. I glance toward Massio, and he gives his head a shake. He doesn't believe it either.

"I-I'm a Christian, sir. I'm saving myself for

marriage." My eyes widen at his admission, and Massio chokes on a laugh. Then the little punk lifts his hand. "I- it's my purity ring, it symbolizes—"

"I know what the fuck a purity ring is," I bellow, causing him to shrink back.

Massio pinches the bridge of his nose. "Jesus fucking Christ. A purity ring?" His wide eyes meet mine, and we stare at one another with confusion.

"Sir, Gracie's father kept her locked up in the house, she was never allowed out. I didn't even know she had a baby until I saw her here. I was truly shocked, sir."

I stroke over my lip, contemplating his words.

"Sir, I don't think the kid is the father. Do you?" Massio eyes me with uncertainty and rolls his lips, probably unsure whether to speak or not, and in this moment, I'm grateful for his silence. I allow the kid to fall to the floor.

Pieces of the puzzle are slowly slipping into place.

"He said he wanted leverage."

Massio nods.

"He said he wanted leverage, Massio!" I say louder as the clouds of jealousy that have consumed me clear, allowing me to think straight. "She's mine."

"Sir?"

A deep-seated agony pulsates in the pit of my stomach as I keel over, and with my fists planted on the wall, I take deep breaths. "Holy fuck. Bonnie. She's mine."

My heart sinks to my feet as her betrayal slices through me.

"Holy shit," Massio chokes out.

DOMINATION

The kid's hand rests on my arm. "Sir, congratulations on becoming a daddy." Congratulations? On becoming a fucking daddy? I shake my head, the kid can't know the meaning behind his words, but fuck me do they hurt anyhow.

She stole her from me.

"Please bring them home safely. I'll pray for their return." I want to scoff at this kid's ignorance, but there's something about his words that I pick up on.

Striding toward the door, I rip it open, Massio hot on my heels. "I know where she is!" I shout.

We bypass a sobbing Hazel and head outside toward the SUV.

"Care to share?" Massio asks.

I stop on the steps of the community center to face my right-hand man. "She's gone home, Massio." His brow furrows as he thinks over my words. "Her old home."

"Why the fuck?"

"The one she grew up in," I clarify. "The ranch."

My little pet has returned home, but when I find her, I'll be sure to keep her on a tighter leash. Her owner is coming to collect her, and when I do, I'll punish her for every betrayal, starting with why the fuck she kept my baby from me.

Chapter Thirty-Nine

Vinny

My thoughts are consumed with Bonnie on the way to the ranch. The way her momma cares for her is what makes me love her all the more. She's everything I would have wanted for my boys, and I couldn't have asked for a more perfect mother than the one she is.

It's what is keeping my anger at bay. I'm barely holding it together, but their safety is paramount to me, so until I have them back in our home, I refuse to give in to the darkness inside me. But she will receive it; every fucking inch of her will receive it. It's clear I've been too gentle on my little pet, treated her with such tenderness she's forgotten who owns her.

As we turn into the ranch, I lean forward and take in the rolling hills. This place is secluded. I'd have security on the gate, brick guard houses, and electric fencing.

The ground crunches beneath the tires as we roll up the driveway. The wraparound porch makes me want to roll my eyes at how quintessential this little hidden gem is.

A man standing at the doorway to the house looks our way, and I wince when Gracie's distraught expression comes into view. I drag a hand through my hair. Shit, this is going to be harder than I anticipated.

"Good luck," Massio grunts as I step out of the SUV and head toward them.

My anger dissipates with the tears streaming down my girl's cheeks. Her chest rises rapidly, and she looks two seconds away from having a full-blown panic attack.

A strangled wail leaves her throat, and her eyes widen on my approach. Bonnie cries out for me, lifting her arms in my direction as she tries to scramble out of Gracie's arms, and that does something to me. Seeing my girls in such anguish has me wanting to right the world of every damn wrong ever committed.

"What's the problem?" I turn toward the man holding onto the door like it's his lifeline.

"She won't leave," he grunts.

"Vi-Vinny, I have the papers. I have papers for the ranch, it's mine." Gracie sobs uncontrollably.

"Lady, I told you before and I'll tell you again, this isn't your damn ranch. I purchased it over a year ago."

Another wail erupts from her.

"Papa!" Bonnie cries as she wrestles to get out of Gracie's arms.

I step forward and hold my arms out for Bonnie, and she shocks the shit out of me by lunging forward, causing Gracie to stumble. I grip her arm to right her, and the devastation swimming in her eyes has me wanting to profess my undying love for her. I want her to tell me she chooses me, she wants me, Mafia life be damned.

But as the sounds of the nature filter through my senses, I know the chances of her choosing the life I can offer are slim. Am I really prepared to pull her away from everything she's ever wanted? How will she truly ever be happy? Satisfied with me. Will she always crave the freedom she so desperately needs?

"I have the papers," she whispers, and I snatch them from her hand, pissed she chose this before me. Took my daughter from me. Lied to me. Betrayed me.

I turn them over somehow while rocking Bonnie from side to side with hopes to settle her.

My eyes scan over the paperwork, and I don't know what the fuck Gracie thinks this is, but all I see are her signatures signing the property deeds over to her father.

A heavy huff leaves me, and I turn my attention toward the prick in the doorway. "Can you give us five?"

"Sure." He slams the door, and I hear the lock engage.

Great.

Gracie falls to the floor in a heap, her sobs are barely contained as she tucks her knees under her, the action making her appear smaller than ever. I lower myself to the floor and sit on the porch step.

"Come." My tone somehow remains calm, and I pat my lap. With Bonnie resting on my hip, Gracie crawls into my lap, and my arm bands around her to hold her in place.

"I'm going to ask you some questions, and you're going to tell me the truth, Gracie."

I breathe in her peach scent, the realization that I may never have smelled her again causes a crushing feeling inside my chest.

"I promise," she whispers, sniffling.

"You lied to me."

"I'm sorry." Her shoulders bunch as she cries deeper into my chest, clinging to my shirt. "I'm so sorry."

"You kept my baby from me, Gracie."

"I didn't want to. I swear it."

"But you fucking did," I snipe out, unable to help myself.

Bonnie presses her finger to my mouth, and my rage there a second ago is eradicated by her soft touch to my lips. "Papa," she mumbles, and her head falls to my shoulder and her eyes close. I place a kiss on my little girl's forehead.

"You didn't think I was worthy." I keep my tone low despite wanting to shout.

Gracie's head pops up from my chest to face me. Her eyes are red and full of anguish and utter devastation. Full of pain. I want to take it away and replace it with nurture.

"Of course, I do." She closes her eyes, and when she reopens them, she straightens her shoulders. "When my mom passed away, I was sent to live with my father. He wasn't kind, Vinny." I nod in understanding. "Then one day he declared he wasn't going to sell my virginity like he'd always tormented me with. I was ecstatic, I thought he'd seen the light." A humorless laugh leaves her. "He told me I had to go to a Halloween party and sleep with the man in the photo he gave me. He said he'd be watching, and he'd know." She licks her lips, then her cheeks heat. "When I saw your picture, I knew I'd rather sleep with you than the men he brought to the house. He said if I did that, he would give me the deeds to the ranch my mother left me in her will."

She glances up at the house behind us, and another tear leaves her. "He was always moving the goal posts, and when I realized I was pregnant, he was really nice to me. For the first time in my life, he was nice." I can see the need for affection radiating from her, and my fingers find her silky hair to give her just that, and my touch gives her the strength to continue on. "He said he wanted to help me with the pregnancy, and he did. He was good." She nods several times like she's convincing herself of her words.

"You didn't think to inform me," I grit out.

"My father said you were dangerous, that he discovered you were a part of the Mafia. He changed when I had Bonnie. He was mean, but he wasn't abusive." I scoff at her words, locking her in a fucking basement is abusive. How can she not see that? "He said I needed to stay at your house until he was out of rehab, then he would bring us back to the ranch. But I had no intentions of waiting. I knew the moment the opportunity arose, I'd take it and come home. I just didn't think it would be so difficult to leave you, and the longer I stayed, the harder it was to leave."

"But you left," I grind out. "You left and took my little girl, Gracie."

"You never would have let me leave if you knew."

"Damn fucking right I wouldn't."

"I-I just want to be free, Daddy. And safe, I want to be safe, and I want Bonnie to have the childhood I did. The freedom I grew up with. The childhood I had."

"You can't read." I don't know why I bite that out; is it below the belt and cruel? Yes, but given the circumstances, I have every right to use it. How the fuck dare she think this life is a better one than the one I can offer. Still, the niggling feeling of her being right has my shoulders falling.

"I have dyslexia, Vinny."

My laugh lacks amusement as I shake my head. "You shouldn't have signed the contract, Little Pet. You didn't know what the hell you were signing."

"I didn't care," she replies with steely determination. "I wanted you." Wanted?

A lump of foreign emotion gathers in my mouth, making it difficult for me to swallow.

"I love you, Vinny. Leaving you made today the worst day of my life. But I needed to do this even if I have failed." She looks back at the farmhouse. "He sold it, didn't he?"

"He did," I confirm, and the guilt that lances through my chest is an odd sensation. "I'm sorry," I say, even though I'm unsure why. I'm not the one who has kept secrets from her and stole the first months of my child's life, stole the chance for me to see her pregnant with my child, but I find myself wanting to comfort her, make everything right.

Bonnie's head springs up from my bicep, and she points to something. "Swing, mamma."

Gracie stares at the apple tree, with a forlorn look

shimmering in her eyes. "My mamma used to push me on that swing. Shall we go see?" She slides off my lap and holds her hand out for Bonnie, and I watch as she carries her toward the swing. Then she scoots her ass onto the swing and maneuvers Bon-Bon onto her lap. The breeze blows Gracie's hair, and the soft giggle Bonnie emits lights up her angelic face with each motion.

As I step toward them, my heart constricts. Can I really do this to them? Take away their freedom.

"Time to go home," I grunt out, motioning toward the SUV. Gracie's shoulders slump, and she gives the farmhouse one final glance before sliding off the swing with Bonnie in her arms.

A lone tear trickles down her cheek, and I step up to swipe it away with the tip of my thumb before sucking it into my mouth.

"You need punished, Little Pet," I mumble for her ears only, kissing her neck.

Her blue eyes light up, and her pupils flare with expectation. "Yes, Daddy," she says as smooth as silk. "I'm ready."

Truth be told, I think it's me who isn't ready.

Chapter Forty

Gracie

Seeing the look of pure devastation on Vinny's face as he said I didn't think he was good enough had me wanting to throw myself at his feet and beg for forgiveness. But right now, as we stand in my bedroom, I know he needs retribution. He wants to punish me for the pain he's suffered and was going to suffer for the rest of his life without us.

"I don't want you to go easy on me, I know you've been holding back." His eyebrows shoot up. "I want you to remember all the things that pissed you off about me, I want you to punish me for stealing your baby, for betraying you and hurting you."

"Gracie," he warns, but I shake my head.

"I mean it. Make me never forget, force me to stay."

"You are staying." His tone is deadly, and a shudder rushes down my spine.

I tuck my hair behind my ear. "Punish me for leaving." As my fingers work the buttons on my blouse, I decide to push him further. "I was going to express my milk."

His nostrils flare and the vein on his neck protrudes. "It's my fucking milk, and you damn well know it."

"I don't know if anyone else would be interested in drinking it." That was definitely the wrong thing to say, or the right, depending on how you look at it. He flies forward and grips me by the throat.

"I don't think you're ready for what Daddy wants to do to you, Little Pet."

"Maybe I should ask—" He launches me on the bed, causing me to bounce on the mattress. Then he unbuckles his belt, grabs a hold of my leggings, and tears them down my legs.

"Look at those little girlie panties. Have you shown them to anyone?" I shake my head. "Has anyone seen them but me?" He doesn't even open the buttons of his shirt, he simply tears it from his body, then drops his pants, and his heavy cock springs free.

"No. I haven't."

He descends on me, grabbing me by my collar, and tugs me up. "Are you lying? Like when you promised you wouldn't leave me?"

My heart pounds against my chest, and I shake my head. His gaze flicks over my face like he's contemplating his next move. "What's your safe word?"

"Red."

His hands snap out, and he grabs my wrists, forcing them behind my back. Then he takes his belt and threads it through my collar and wraps it around my wrists, binding me. Next, he throws me onto my stomach, causing my core to clench at his heavy-handedness. "Please, I need you to punish me, Daddy."

"Damn fucking right you do," he seethes. His voice is so deadly it sends a delightful ripple of fear through my entire body. "You need me to wash away your sins, don't you, Little Pet." Something in his tone sends a wave of anticipation through me, and when I hear his zipper lower, I clench my thighs together, waiting on bated breath for his next move.

Vinny

Standing at the edge of the bed, I revel her lying on her stomach with the belt around her neck and her innocent panties on. Which doesn't dissipate the monster inside me, it only feeds it, and the way the scent of her arousal fills the air has my cock harder than ever before.

My nostrils widen with each controlled breath I take; my veins protrude with the simmering blood rushing through me like lava, and my fists flex as I mumble the words out. "Last chance to say your safe word, *Little Pet*." I spit out the latter like poison on my tongue.

"I'm yours. Punish me," she pants out, thrashing on the bed as if searching for me.

Her words stir the demon, bringing it to the surface. The darkness that consumes me will now consume her. I only hope she can forgive me when I cleanse her of her sins.

I grab a hold of her panties and tear them, leaving her bare to me. Then I grab the belt and drag her to the floor. Her eyes fly open, her pupils widening, and her entire body tenses with my rough handling of her. When I aim my cock on her back, it's like a switch has been flicked, her taut body relaxes, and I clench my teeth and aim my piss at her. "You'll take this." I bare my teeth. "Let Daddy wash away your sins, Little Pet." The sight of it splashing against her perfect skin is intoxicating. "Let him punish you," I groan.

Pissing while your cock is hard is difficult but not impossible, and I've had plenty of practice, but nothing compares to watching my girl rub her cunt against the floor while I deliver a warm stream of piss on her.

It's degrading, it's filthy, and the pleasure is euphoric.

Before I finish, I push open her thighs and position myself behind her. Placing the tip of my cock at her pussy, I open my bladder again. "Holy fuck. Holy fuck, Little Pet." I harden further at the sight, my piss filling her hole.

Jesus, this is going to feel good when I slide inside her. Filthy her up, giving me the perfect excuse to clean her.

A gasp leaves her. "Does that feel good, Daddy pissing inside you?" I pant.

As soon as I'm finished pissing, I jerk my cock frantically at her entrance. Like a feral animal, I grab the belt, uncaring of it biting into her skin, and pin her to the floor by her neck, mounting her like a beast.

My cock glides through her slickness, and my eyes roll when I slide inside her warm, wet heat. Could she be any more perfect? She loves this depravity as much as I do. "Filthy, Little Pet," I admonish. Her pussy clenches, and I chuckle as the piss flows down my cock.

DOMINATION

Slam.

My fingers wrap around her neck so tight it causes her eyes to bulge, but I don't stop, each powerful thrust harder than the last. Without warning, I shove two fingers into her ass, and her spine arches, her lips part, and a gargled sound leaves her lips, unable to make any coherent sound other than that of choking. Absolute pure satisfaction licks up my spine as my balls draw up. "I'm going to ruin you, Little Pet," I snipe out, and electric sparks explode inside me. "I own you now." I thrust deeper, and her pussy clamps around my cock, making each surge more and more intense. "Fuck. Fuck!" My slit widens, every nerve ending alive with pure ecstasy as her body falls lax and my cum fills her cunt, every fucking part of me consuming her.

Chapter Forty-One

Gracie

My mouth is sore, my lips tender, and I whimper as I lift my head, allowing his cock to slip from my mouth.

"Shhh, it's okay, Little Pet. You did so good for Daddy."

"T-thank you."

His lip lifts, and he holds his hands out for me to climb up his body, and each movement has me wincing. Last night, I blacked out, but I know he used me how he needed to; he finally gave me his all, and I gave him mine.

He sits up, with me straddling his lap. "Come, drink this." He holds a bottle of water to my mouth, and I swallow it back, then his thumb tenderly swipes at my lips. "Open," he grunts, then places a pill on my tongue. "Pain relief. You had some during the night, but I don't want you to suffer any more than you already have."

"I don't mind," I whisper, and he lifts the bottle to my mouth again, allowing me to swallow back the pill.

"I'm sorry about last night." Guilt swims in his dark eyes, and I hate it. His fingers graze over the redness on my wrists from where the belt was bound around me. "I bathed you and covered you in lotion." His fingers massage my thighs as though he's reliving his actions. "I washed your hair." He strokes my hair. "I fed from your tits." Instead of squeezing my breasts, he brushes over them with the pads of his fingers. "All while I prayed for you to be pregnant." His hand finally comes to a stop on my stomach and so do his eyes. "That way you'd need me to care for you, and I get to watch you grow. That way you never leave me."

"I need you now, Vinny."

"Do you?" He lifts an eyebrow. "I devoured your body last night like a savage, Gracie. I've killed men for less."

"I consented, and besides, I liked it."

"I fucked you while you slept," he says, possibly thinking that would make a difference to my feelings toward him.

"Good. I wish I wasn't on birth control."

His head shoots up to lock eyes with mine and his pupils flare, but I ignore his reaction and continue on. "I hope I'm pregnant with your baby, Daddy. I never want to leave you again, you're ours."

His chest heaves, and the way his stare darkens, I can tell he likes that. I lower my head so my lips almost touch his. "I love you, Vinny, Daddy, Papa, and I never want to leave you. I'm only sorry I did." He sucks in a sharp breath, then slams his lips against mine, our tongues tangle and my hands weave into his silver hair as I grind my body against his.

When he pulls me back by my arms, I'm breathless, my body thrumming with desire. He slides from beneath me, taking me by surprise.

He doesn't look at me as he starts getting dressed, and that stuns me more than him leaving me in bed with an aching need for him.

Marching toward the door, he shocks the hell out of me. "There's something I need to do."

The slam behind him has me deflating, and I bite into my lip, wishing I could take back every move I made that destroyed the man I love. But I wouldn't change a thing about last night.

None of it.

Chapter Forty-Two

Vinny

All day, the disappointment on her pretty face has flashed in front of my mind, taunting me.

The door closes behind Tommy, and I wait for him to take a seat, then I stub out my cigar.

"You've been notably absent again," Rafael spits out, his glare seething with rage. "We tidied up the mess, thank you for asking."

"Papa, did you lose your way home? You need one of those tracker things you can have around your neck that you press if you need assistance." I blink at Rocco. "Saw it on TV." He shrugs.

"Do you have one for your wife?" Tommy quips, making me chuckle.

"Shut the fuck up. Least I didn't raid a high school for a fuck."

"You kind of did though." Tommy grins back with a smug smile. He's not wrong. Rocco's wife was his teacher.

"I did, didn't I?" He beams.

"Are you even going to ask what the hell happened yesterday?" Rafael glares. "Why have you even called us here if you're not interested?"

I sit up straighter. "I have news."

"Is it your prostate?" Rocco asks, then he lifts up two fingers. "You know there's a walnut inside ..."

Tommy swipes at the back of his head, saving me the energy.

"Well, in case you're interested, it was Darryl Davis that called Jade, tipping us off."

"What?" I frown in confusion.

"Turns out the little punk wants rid of his grandfather too," Rafael states.

"Interesting," I muse, tapping my finger against my lip.

"Even more interesting is he wants to work for us."

I lift my eyebrows; just because the punk helped us out, doesn't mean he can be trusted. Maybe it was a ploy to lower our defenses, to welcome him in so he can spy.

"We can't trust him yet," Rafael says, confirming my suspicions. "But I do have a job for him."

"Go on."

"I'm going to suggest he goes undercover with the MC linked to the O'Connells, as a prospect. Then he can find the link and prove his worth."

Proud. That's what I am. Proud.

I smirk, knowing what I'm about to do has made my decision even easier.

"Why the hell are you smiling like a loon? Is the

DOMINATION

prostate? Are you sick?" Rafael fires one question after the other.

"No." I swat my hand in his direction, clearing my throat. "I'm a father again. Bonnie is mine. Biologically, I mean."

"She was anyway," Rafael states with a lift of his shoulder as if I didn't just confirm he has another blood sibling. "Congratulations." There's no malice or patronizing tone, he genuinely means his words, and I nod at him before looking at my other two sons.

"I got a little sister. Cute. Can you tell her that her niece might have some dresses she can have that she's grown out of." Rocco grins cockily.

"She can have her own fucking dresses," I bite back.

"We're pleased for you, Papa." Tommy nods.

"I take it you're going to marry her?" Rafael states.

"Of course."

"So you brought us here to tell us the good news." His dark eyes hold mine, and I don't miss the tic in his jaw. He thinks I'm not interested in what went down at the warehouse, but of course I am, I do after all have Robert to deal with.

"Actually, that was just the start." I hold his stare, and his lips part, but I hold my hand up, making Rocco cough on a laugh. "I'm retiring. I'm handing the reins over to you. I'm proud of you, Rafael, and I couldn't think of anyone more suitable for the position." Shock stuns him silent, his eyes widen, and his Adam's apple slowly works down his throat. This is what he's been trained for, preened and prepared for his entire life. He probably thought this day would never come, not until my deathbed at least.

"Congratulations, brother." Rocco slaps him on the back while Tommy's smile spreads across his face, the pride in it evident.

"Are you sure?" Rafael splutters. "What are you going to do?"

I take a deep breath and slowly roam my gaze over each of them. "I'm going to raise my girls the way I should have raised you boys." The way their faces soften and their shoulders relax tell me they understand. They are, after all, the men I've always wanted to be. "But right now, I'm going to take my girls home." I push back in my chair and stride toward the door.

"Home?" Tommy queries as I shut the door behind me.

Home.

Chapter Forty-Three

Vinny

She leans her head against the window of the SUV, her eyes blindfolded. Massio's gaze bounces back and forth from mine to the road like he's unsure of what I'm doing. Bonnie is asleep, a snoozing sound leaving her little lips, causing a bubble of spittle to gather with each breath she takes. I trace over the soft skin of her chubby hand, relishing the feeling of knowing she's mine, truly mine.

When the SUV comes to a stop, I make quick work of my seatbelt and head around to Gracie's side of the vehicle. I lift her into my arms, and she squeals while swatting at me. "Vinny!"

"Shhh, don't wake our daughter, not yet," I mumble against her ear, and her body relaxes. Jesus, I love saying that. I always considered having girls a weakness, but now, I can think of nothing more incredible than having the beauty and innocence of multiple Gracies running around.

I slide her down my body until her feet touch the floor. Then with her back against my chest, I slide the blindfold off her eyes. The moment she realizes where she is, her breath catches and her legs buckle, but I band my arm around her to keep her upright.

"Welcome home, Little Pet." I smile brightly and glance over her shoulder toward the ranch.

There're two horses in the paddock beside the barn; there's a fucking chicken coop for Christ sake, and a swinging bench on the porch that I intend on her sucking me on every evening as the sun goes down.

Hazel will move in with us and continue with helping keep the house while maintaining her relationship with the girls.

She spins to face me. "Wh-what?" Tears swim in her eyes.

"I bought the ranch back. It's ours. We're going to live here." I glance over my shoulder at the property. It didn't take much to negotiate a deal. Throw in the fact I informed him of who I was, and the guy practically threw the keys at me. "But we're having security on the gate," I tack on.

"V-Vinny, you're not making any sense." Hope bounces in her gaze as she scans my face.

I take her face in the palms of my hands. "You're my home, Gracie. Wherever you are, I am. Your heart is here, then so is mine."

"But the Mafia." Her lip quivers.

"Is all Rafael's. He's more than capable. It took you to

make me see it." I swipe the tears from her cheeks. "I want to be the father I should have been. The husband you deserve. The owner of a little pet who would never have a reason to leave me."

She shakes her head. "I won't. I wouldn't."

"I know you won't. You no longer have a cage, Little Pet. Now you're finally free."

A sob catches in her throat, and she launches herself toward me.

"Now you're home," I whisper against the silky locks of her hair. "And so am I."

Epilogue

Vinny

He's on a piss-stained mattress, covered in dried blood from the cuts that litter his body. His fingertips and toes are missing, his teeth too. He's probably wishing for death, and while I've spent the past eight months watching my wife grow my baby, I'll keep him alive another ten months. The exact amount of time he kept Gracie and Bonnie from me.

Slowly, we will torture him to death, taking him piece by piece.

"Please, just kill me." His words are barely audible.

"You need to pay for your sins," I drawl out, settling beside Massio.

When we realized Robert planned on using my daughter as leverage, he just made things for himself so much worse. Before, I was simply going to torture him to death, now, I intended to brutalize him, return him to the brink of good health and repeat the process over and fucking over again.

The past six months, Massio has been at the ranch as head of security, but I can feel the dissatisfaction from him a mile away. He likes action, after all, it's not like he's in retirement too.

I nudge him with my shoulder. "I have a job for you."

He huffs and rolls his neck toward me. "The horse bolt again?" he snarks.

"No, actually. It's this." I lift the folded photo from my pocket and hand it over to him. "Rafael suggested it. When I told him you were getting angsty."

"Fucking angsty? Bored, you mean," he clips, making my eyebrows furrow. It seems it's only me and my girls who appreciate the seclusion of the ranch.

"Open it." I gesture.

He unfolds the photo, then jolts when he sees who it is. A young woman, the mirror image of her mother—his ex-wife, the one who broke his heart and soul. "She needs a bodyguard," I quip with a smirk. "The job is yours if you want it." He stares at the photo, and anger flashes over his face. "Be warned, apparently, she's a brat that needs taming. Maybe she needs a daddy." I wink, and fire flares in his eyes. I stand and button up my jacket, and a wail sounds from Robert as Rocco slices off a portion of skin, and when I step through the door, it's with certainty.

Massio will be leaving us. He's about to cage his own little pet. I just hope the little brat is ready to be tamed. Something tells me Massio will be doing it anyway.

Gracie

Vinny text to say he was on his way home and I should be in our bedroom naked and waiting for him like a good little pet.

My stomach touches the carpet as I bow on the floor. At eight months pregnant, I'm not sure how it happened after Vinny had a doctor administer birth control. But we're both happy, and better yet, he hasn't been able to leave me alone. He's obsessed with my bump, loving nothing more than to lotion it up and kiss and caress it while he drinks my milk.

"Such a good little pet for Daddy." The click of the bathroom door tells me he showered before stepping into the bedroom. Something he does often when returning from seeing his sons.

Although Vinny would never admit it to me, I'm sure he hasn't fully stepped away from the Mafia, but do they ever? All I care about is him coming home every night and waking up to him every morning. Preferably with my lips around his cock while he soothes me with methodical strokes of my hair.

The mattress dips when he takes a seat. "Come." He pats his lap, and I crawl over to him, then he helps me up from the floor. His calloused hand brings my nipple to his mouth, and he sucks hard, stealing the air from my lungs. "Hmm," he grunts, and slickness gathers between my thighs. "All swollen and full for Daddy." He detaches, and a stream of milk spills out of the corner of his mouth. "Have you been saving your milk up for me, Little Pet?"

"Yes," I pant. Bonnie has stopped breastfeeding, so now it's all for Vinny, much to his delight.

"Good girl, spin and face the mirror." He helps me turn on his lap, then positions me so my legs are straddling his, opening me up to the mirror.

"Oh, god." I moan as he swipes his fingers over my slick folds, causing my back to arch.

"Spray your milk on my fingers," he growls while kissing up my neck, sending a flurry of goose bumps over me.

Pinching my nipple, I coat his fingers in my warm milk, then he moves them between my legs and slides one finger then the other inside my ass, scissoring them when he pushes past my tightness. "Good Little Pet, opening her ass up to Daddy and his thick cock."

I throw my head back on his shoulder when he positions the tip of his cock at my entrance. "Watch Daddy stretch you wide," he breathes into my ear. "Watch Daddy push inside your tiny ass, Little Pet." My eyes latch on to the action in the mirror. The stretch of his cock against my tight muscle is full of pain coupled with pleasure. His free hand moves to thrum my clit, and I push down on his thickness with each stroke of my swollen bud. He hisses through his teeth, then, as if unable to help himself, he bites into my skin, and I cry out before slamming myself down, taking him all inside me. He moves his hands to rove over my protruding stomach. "You did so well making a baby for Daddy," he grunts, and I dig my fingernails into his thighs to push up and down on him, fucking him with vigor while he switches between caressing my bump and toying with my milky nipples.

The sight in the mirror is erotic, full of splendor, admiration, and love.

It's a beautiful torment.
It's home.

THE END

Massio sneak peek ...

Massio

Vinny hands me the photo and I flinch when I see who it is.

At least at first, I think it's her.

The woman that destroyed me, and the thought has my chest seizing up making it difficult for me to breathe and I briefly close my eyes before snapping them open, determined to not let her have this power over me once again.

I knew she'd moved on. Fuck, did I know about it. She promised me the world then threw me out like trash for a wealthier option.

It was only obvious she'd end up pregnant with heirs in order to cement her claim in society.

Still, seeing it hurts.

My mouth is dry as I scan the photo, on further inspection I can see the differences, this girl is smaller framed, heavier breasted but just as stunning, if not more

Massio sneak peek ...

so. "She needs a bodyguard," Vinny smirks and my eyebrows shoot up. "The job is yours if you want it." A mix of emotions combine, fury at the life she went on to lead without me, followed by the feeling of excitement at the thought of retribution. "Be warned, apparently, she's a brat that needs taming. Maybe she needs a daddy." His words hang in the air and my cock thickens in my slacks.

The prospect of punishing my ex-wife while filling her daughter with my thick cum has pure need rushing through me like a drug.

I want that.

I want that more than anything.

I've no idea how to tame a brat.

But I'm going to have fun doing it.

The Mafia Daddies Series will continue with Massio and his family.

Preorder UNTAMED.

Acknowledgments

Tee the lady that started it all for me. Thank you for an eternity.

I must start with where it all began, TL Swan. When I started reading your books, I never realized I was in a place I needed pulling out of. Your stories brought me back to myself.

With your constant support and the network created as 'Cygnet Inkers' I was able to create something I never realized was possible, I genuinely thought I'd had my day. You made me realize tomorrow is just the beginning.

<u>**SPECIAL MENTION**</u>

To Jo, thank you for being on this journey with me. I appreciate everything you do, every message you send and all your support. I feel blessed to have you, thank you.

Jaclyn, thank you for being you. You're always there if I need you, and for that, I am truly grateful.

Acknowledgments

Lilibet, thank you for all your support, your thoughts and suggestions are amazing. I appreciate you hun.

Terra thank you for being on board, your support and messages mean the world.

A huge shout out to Vicky B, Debbie and Elsa. You ladies give me so much encouragement with your enthusiasm. I appreciate everything you do to support me. Thank you.

My Incredible ARC and Street Teams.

Your messages, shares, reviews and support is incredible. I'm incredibly grateful and forever in awe. Thank you for everything.

Book Besties

Thank you both for all your support. I hope you love Vinny as much as I did writing him.

My Reckless Readers!

THANK YOU!

Reckless Readers is my happy place, thank you for helping build it and being a part of it.

To my world.

To my boys, I hope you never read this acknowledgment, it means you probably read the book. Let's not go there.

To my hubby, the J in my BJ.

What an amazing hubby you are. Thank you for keeping me sane. I love and appreciate you.

Without you I wouldn't be BJ Alpha. Love you trillions!

And finally…

Thank you to you, my readers.
Thank you for helping make my dreams a reality.
Love Always
BJ Alpha. X

More...

How would you like an insight into Bren's story?
Click on the link for a sneak peek: BREN

About the Author

BJ Alpha lives in the UK with her hubby, two teenage sons and three fur babies.
She loves to write and read about hot, alpha males and feisty females.

Follow me on my social media pages:
Facebook: BJ Alpha
My readers group: BJ's Reckless Readers
Instagram: BJ Alpha

Also by BJ Alpha

SECRETS AND LIES SERIES
CAL Book 1
CON Book 2
FINN Book 3
BREN Book 4
OSCAR Book 5
CON'S WEDDING NOVELLA
O'CONNELL'S FOREVER

BORN SERIES
BORN RECKLESS

THE BRUTAL DUET
HIDDEN IN BRUTAL DEVOTION
LOVE IN BRUTAL DEVOTION

THE BRUTAL DUET PART TWO
BRUTAL SECRETS
BRUTAL LIES

STORM ENTERPRISES
SHAW Book 1
TATE Book 2

OWEN Book 3

REED Book 4

VEILED IN SERIES

VEILED IN HATE

CARRERA FAMILY

STONE

MAFIA DADDIES

DADDY'S ADDICTION Book 1

POSSESSION Book 2

DECEPTION Book 3

DOMINATION Book 4

UNTAMED Book 5